History
of
Bourbon County, Kansas,

to the
Close of 1865

T. F. Robley

HERITAGE BOOKS
2025

HERITAGE BOOKS
AN IMPRINT OF HERITAGE BOOKS, INC.

Books, CDs, and more—Worldwide

For our listing of thousands of titles see our website
at
www.HeritageBooks.com

A Facsimile Reprint
Published 2025 by
HERITAGE BOOKS, INC.
Publishing Division
5810 Ruatan Street
Berwyn Heights, MD 20740

Copyright © 1894 T. F. Robley, Fort Scott, Kansas

— Publisher's Notice —
In reprints such as this, it is often not possible to remove
blemishes from the original. We feel the contents of this
book warrant its reissue despite these blemishes and
hope you will agree and read it with pleasure.

International Standard Book Number
Paperbound: 978-0-7884-2772-5

INTRODUCTION

IN preparing this book I have departed in many particulars from the ordinary course and established custom of compilers of county histories. I have endeavored to give the causes which led up to our early troubles, and to delineate, to some extent, the public sentiment and feeling of given periods. I have kept in touch with the various Territorial Governments, Administrations, Legislatures and prominent public men, in order that the reader may have an intelligent understanding of the situation. I have intended this book to be of refreshing interest to the old settler, and to be especially interesting and instructive to the young men and women of Bourbon County.

T. F. ROBLEY.

FORT SCOTT, KANSAS, *December, 1894.*

SYNOPTICAL INDEX.

PAGE

CHAPTER I.—Louisiana Purchase—Missouri Territory—Missouri Compromise—Platte Purchase—Santa Fe Trail—Cherokee Neutral Lands—New York Indian Lands 8

CHAPTER II.—Fort Scott Located—Colonel H. T. Wilson—Sergeant John Hamilton—Military Road Completed—Barracks Erected—Relics of a Past Era...................... 17

CHAPTER III.—Annexation of Texas—Mexican War—Wilmot Proviso—Compromise of 1850 21

CHAPTER IV.—1853—Post of Fort Scott Abandoned—Some of the Early Settlers of Bourbon County—Time from 1854 to 1855—Description of Frontier Life—Climate—Indian Summer.. 29

CHAPTER V.—1854—Mill of the Gods—Kansas-Nebraska Bill —Kansas Territory Organized........................... 33

CHAPTER VI.—1854—First Governor—First Elections—First Fraud—First Legislature—Bogus Statutes—Samples of Legislation—Government Buildings Sold 42

CHAPTER VII.—1855—Bourbon County Organized—First County Officers—Neutral Lands in Bourbon County—Fort Scott Incorporated as a Town—More Elections—Second Governor—Political Atmosphere of Bourbon County...... 53

CHAPTER VIII.—1856—Tone of Pro-slavery Papers—Topeka Constitution—Trouble Commences—Texas Rangers—Expedition to Middle Creek—Topeka Legislature—Governor Shannon Resigns—Governor Geary Appointed—Territorial Legislators for Bourbon County—Close of 1856........... 60

CHAPTER IX.—1857.—Bourbon County Officials—New Towns —Sprattsville—Mapleton—Rayville—Means of Communication... 64

SYNOPTICAL INDEX.

PAGE

CHAPTER X.—1857—Some More Politics—Dred Scott Decision—Slaves in Bourbon County—Governor Geary Resigns—Governor Walker Appointed—More Immigrants—Fort Scott Town Company—U. S. Officers—Tenderfeet—Free State Hotel.. 77

CHAPTER XI.—1857— Public Sentiment —Lecompton Constitution— Election of October 5, 1857 — More Trouble— Squatter's Court—Protective Society...................... 86

CHAPTER XII.—1857—The Conservatives—U. S. Troops at Fort Scott—First Election on Lecompton Constitution— Close of 1857.......... 90

CHAPTER XIII.—1858—The Second Election on Lecompton Constitution—First Newspaper Established - First Grand Ball—Trouble Begins Again—Object Lesson in Surgery— Origin of Jayhawker...................................... 96

CHAPTER XIV.—1858—First Manufactory in Fort Scott—Marmaton Town Company—Uniontown—Leavenworth Constitution—English Bill—Jayhawking Reduced to Plain Stealing—Fight with U. S. Troops.. 104

CHAPTER XV.—1858—Some Old Settlers of 1858—Improvements Begin—Border Ruffians have an Inning—Marais des Cygnes Murder—Efforts at Capture—Effects on the Border —Feeling Against Fort Scott........................... 114

CHAPTER XVI.—1858—Public Meeting—Election by "Tailment"—Meeting at Rayville—Protocol of Peace—Montgomery Sized Up.... 119

CHAPTER XVII.—1858—Some More Arrivals—After the Amnesty—Improvements Continue—Exit Lecompton Constitution—Kansas is Free.... 125

CHAPTER XVIII.—1858—Territorial Election—Governor Denver Resigns—Samuel Medary Appointed—Amnesty Broken —Ben Rice Arrested—Meeting at Rayville—Release of Rice —Death of John H. Little..... 133

CHAPTER XIX.—1859—Militia Organized—Jayhawkers Captured—Lawrence and Fort Scott get Acquainted—Amnesty Law—County Seat Moved—Preparing for Another Constitution—An All Around Good Year...................... 141

SYNOPTICAL INDEX.

PAGE

CHAPTER XX.—1859—Delegates to Wyandotte Convention—Big 4th of July—Grand Ball—Fort Scott Democrat Revived—Vote on the Wyandotte Constitution—Other Election Items...... 146

CHAPTER XXI.—1860—Legislature Meets—Dayton Incorporated—Fort Scott Town Company Incorporated—Fort Scott Incorporated as a City—First City Election—County Election—Last Border Difficulties—Law Inaugurated...... 151

CHAPTER XXII.—1860—Arts of Peace—Population—First Fair Association—N. Y. Indian Lands—Neutral Lands—Troops Arrive—Land Sales—The Great Drouth........... 160

CHAPTER XXIII.—1861—Kansas Admitted—State Government—City Affairs—Impending Crisis—Public Meetings—War—War Feeling in Bourbon County—First Troops Organized............ 168

CHAPTER XXIV.—1862—Fort Lincoln Fortified—Troops Concentrated—Battle of Drywood—6th Kansas—Fort Scott a Military Post—More Politics............ 174

CHAPTER XXV.—1862—Movement of Troops—Various Items—Fall Elections............ 178

CHAPTER XXVI.—1863—County Seat Returned to Fort Scott—City Hall—Elections—County Officers............ 182

CHAPTER XXVII.—1864—Political Feeling—Fortifications—Raids on Drywood—Railroads—Politics—Price Raid—Raids by Guerillas—Marmaton Massacre—Fort Scott in Suspense—Public Meeting—General Election............ 198

CHAPTER XXVIII.—1865—Lincoln—City Election—Muster Out—The Schools—Business and Improvements—Fall Election—Statistics—Population—The Close............ 210

Relics of a Past Era.

HISTORY OF
Bourbon County, Kansas.

By T. F. ROBLEY.

CHAPTER I.

THE LOUISIANA PURCHASE.

ONE of the most important events in the history of the United States was the purchase of Louisiana Territory from the Republic of France. The treaty of cession was concluded at Paris on the 30th day of April, 1803, by and between the ministers of President Thomas Jefferson and Napoleon Bonaparte, then First Consul of France. The far-reaching effects of this cession on the future of the whole civilized world, and its immense advantages to the United States as a Nation, can scarcely be realized. By this acquisition the United States added to its territory 1,160,577 square miles to the 820,680 square miles of the original thirteen colonies, for which it paid a sum amounting to less than twenty million dollars. By this acquisition it added a grand inter-oceanic zone, reaching down from the rugged coast of the North Pacific to the crescent shore of the Gulf; down from the regions of eternal snows to the clime of eternal flowers.

The Republic moved at once into its place on the map of the world as a Power of the first class—a Nation with a big N. This was one of the few grand victories won by the pen instead of the sword.

Conceive, if you can, the consequences if President Jefferson, without the authority of Congress or of constitutional law, had failed at the supreme moment to say, in effect, to Bonaparte, "*L'Etat c'est moi.*" "I will take it."

England would undoubtedly have taken it from France as she had successively taken Canada, Cape Breton, New Foundland, Nova Scotia and portions of Asia, and as she finally from Napoleon "wrenched the the sceptre with an unlineal hand." The fear that this territory would ultimately fall into the hands of England, coupled with his great need of money at that time, induced Bonaparte to make the proposition to Jefferson to sell the entire province, just as he had acquired it only a short time previously by retrocession from Spain. And Jefferson, realizing its vital importance to his country, and also the danger of delays, at once closed the bargain on his own responsibility, as has been seen, without the authority of the constitution, which made no provision for incorporating foreign territory, without the authority of Congress, which was not then in session, but by an act as arbitrary and autocratic as could have been done by the Czar of Russia. On that subject Jefferson himself wrote:

"The less that is said about any constitutional difficulty the better. Congress should do what is necessary in silence. I find but one opinion about the necessity of shutting up the Constitution for some time."

Nevertheless, for that act alone, if for no others, future generations of his countrymen will place his statue the very next to Washington's in the line of historic marbles.

The territory was bounded on the east by the Mississippi river south to the 31st parallel—about one degree north of the city of New Orleans—thence east to the Pardido river, which is now the west boundary of Florida. The west country was the east and north boundaries of Texas to the 100th meridian; thence north to the Arkansas river; thence along the Arkansas river to the "divide" of the Rocky Mountains to and along the 106th meridian, to and along the 42nd parallel to the Pacific ocean. The north line being the present boundary between the British Possessions and the United States.

MISSOURI TERRITORY.

In 1812 the territory then known as the Territory of Orleans was admitted into the Union as the State of Louisiana, and by act of Congress in June, 1812, the balance of the Louisiana purchase became the Territory of Missouri. In March, 1819, the Territory of Arkansas was created.

MISSOURI COMPROMISE.

By act of Congress known as the Missouri Compromise, approved March 6th, 1820, the Territory of Missouri was erected with a view of admission as a State.

Section 8 of that act provided that in all territory north of 36 degrees and 30 minutes north latitude, not included within the limits of the contemplated State of Missouri, slavery should be forever prohibited.

PLATTE PURCHASE

The west boundary line of the State of Missouri, as designated by that law, was as it now exists, except that from the mouth of the Kaw river the line ran due north to the Iowa line, instead of the Missouri river forming the boundary as now. This territory between the due north line and the Missouri river was known as the "Platte Purchase." In June, 1836, Congress passed a law adding the Platte Purchase to Missouri, and this tract of land became slave territory, in direct violation of the compromise of 1820.

SANTA FE TRAIL.

By an act of Congress of June, 1825, Major Sibley, of the United States Army, was appointed to survey and establish a wagon road from Independence, Missouri, to Santa Fe, New Mexico, known as the Santa Fe Trail. This was the first highway of civilization to penetrate this then unexplored and silent desert.

And this within the memory of our old men! But we will go into no retrospect here. Get on a Santa Fe train, which passes over subtantially the survey made by Major Sibley, and the retrospect will come to you much more forcibly than it can be written. Consider that, then the valleys of the Kaw, Marias des Cygnes, Neosho, Marmaton and Paint Creek were the favorite hunting grounds of the Osages, Cheyennes and Arapahoes. The wolves, deer, antelope and the migratory buffalo roamed the wild prairie unfettered by wire fence and unbalked by railroad crossing. And that only seventy-five years ago. Even thirty years ago they had not yet departed from the now confines of Wichita's additions.

CHEROKEE NEUTRAL LANDS.

About 1825 the government began locating the various tribes of the more nearly civilized Indians from the East and South on reservations, by cessions, trades, treaties, removals and retrocessions, up to about the year 1852. In 1828 a treaty was made with the Cherokees, of Georgia, by which they were given the territory known as the Cherokee Nation, with a promise also of the payment of $450,000. But this money was never paid them, and in 1835 a supplementary treaty was made by which they were granted, in lieu of said sum of money, a tract of land bounded and described as follows:

"Beginning at the northeast corner of the Cherokee Nation; thence north along the Missouri state line fifty miles; thence west twenty-five miles; thence south fifty miles; thence east to the place of beginning."

This tract, twenty-five by fifty miles was intended to contain 800,000 acres.

This grant has always been known as the "Cherokee Neutral Lands." It is said that the reason it was so called was that the Cherokee Nation was slave territory and the Cherokees being slave holders, they preferred to have neutral ground between their nation and the free territory north of 36° 30', as provided for by the Missouri Compromise. Consequently, instead of the money due by the provisions of the treaty, they chose in lieu thereof this "Neutral Land" as a bulwark against freedom.

As these lands were partly contained in Bourbon County, occasion will be taken to refer to them further along in regular chronological order.

NEW YORK INDIAN LANDS.

On January 15th, 1838, the government set apart to the various tribes of New York Indians a tract of country described as follows:

"Beginning at the west line of the State of Missouri, at the northeast corner of the Cherokee tract and running thence north along the west line of the State of Missouri twenty-seven miles to the southerly line of the Miami lands; thence west so far as shall be necessary by running a line at right angles and parallel to the west line aforesaid to the Osage lands, and thence easterly along the Osage and Cherokee lands to the place of beginning; to include 1,824,000 acres."

This land was intended as a future home for the Indians of New York. These various tribes of New

York Indians, consisting of the remnants of the Senecas, Onondagas, Cayugas, Tuscaroras, Oneidas, St. Regis, Stockbridges, Munsees and Brothertowns, were called the "Six Nations."

As will be seen the balance of what is now Bourbon County was contained within this tract of New York Indian lands.

But it was never occupied by the tribes mentioned, there having been but thirty-two allotments made to them of 320 acres each, which were all on the Osage river.

As this tract was not a grant in fee simple, like that to the Cherokees, but designed to be allotted in severalty to individual members of the tribes, and as only thirty-two of them came west to receive their share, the remainder of the tract finally reverted to the United States.

Lieutenant John C. Fremont in June, 1842, left Chouteau's trading post on the Marias des Cygnes river, in what is now Linn County, on his first expedition to the Rocky Mountains. He was accompanied by Kit Carson as guide.

We now have a clear idea of the condition of things in this country—physically and politically—as they existed in that early day. The United States had acquired a clear and unquestioned title to the domain; many of the tribes of Indians in the Eastern and Southern States, who were in the way of the rapidly increasing population, had been given, and located on, large tracts of land in this worthless, sterile desert, totally unfit for the habitation of the white man, as it was believed, where they could quietly work out their own extinction.

The Nation was on a solid and enduring foundation; peace reigned supreme, and, better than all, the troublesome, vexatious and dangerous question of African slavery had, in the minds of all men, been settled peacefully, finally and forever.

CHAPTER II.

FORT SCOTT LOCATED.

IN the year 1837, by an order of Colonel Zachary Taylor, a military Board of Commissioners, consisting of Colonel S. W. Kearney and Captain Nathan Boone, of the 1st U. S. Dragoons, was appointed to lay out a military road from Fort Coffey in the Cherokee Nation to Fort Leavenworth on the Missouri river, and to select a site for a new Post to be located somewhere nearly midway between those two points, for the accommodation of the garrison at Fort Wayne, a post then existing near the Arkansas line, about fifty miles south of the northeast corner of the Cherokee Nation, which it had been decided to abandon.

In reference to the location of the new post, the commission reported much difficulty in fixing upon a site. Several points were examined along Spring river. Their first choice seems to have been at the place of Joseph Rogers, a Cherokee Indian, living near the present site of Baxter Springs. But Rogers thought he was in the midst of a "boom," and he asked them $1,000 an acre for what land they would need of his claim. They were not authorized to pay any such sum, and considering also that it was more desirable to locate the site on land not granted to Indians, they moved on further north.

Bearing on the question of the selection of a site, a copy is given of a letter from the War Department, as follows:

"MRS. H. T. WILSON,
      Fort Scott, Kansas.

Madam:

Replying to your inquiry of the 6th inst. as to who selected the site of the military post at Fort Scott, Kansas, I have the honor to inform you that the site was selected in 1837 by a Board of Commissioners, charged with the duty of laying out a military road from Fort Coffey to Fort Leavenworth, consisting of Col. S. W. Kearney and Captain Nathan Boone, 1st Dragoons. Their report will be found in H. R. Doc. No. 278, 25th Congress, 2d Session, which report is too lengthy to be copied.

There was some considerable difficulty in fixing the site for the Fort Wayne garrison. The first point selected was at Rogers' place on Spring river, but was abandoned on account of the exorbitant price demanded by its owner. Several other points in the immediate neighborhood, and up the Pomme de Terre or Spring River, to the State line were examined, but decided to be unhealthy. All the several points were examined by Captain Moore, and other sites in that vicinity had been previously examined by General Taylor; and it was only after these different sites had been determined as impracticable, that the position on the Marmaton, which had been previously recommended by the Board in 1837, was finally decided upon as a site for the new post.

I am, Madam, Very Respectfully,
Your Obedient Servant,
J. C. KELTON,
Act'g Ass't Adj't General."

Considerable time was now consumed, presumably in the process of red tape and in construction of the military road from Fort Leavenworth south, so that it was not until the 26th day of May, 1842, when the garrison of Fort Wayne abandoned that post and took up their march for the North. They arrived at the new site which had been selected on the Marmaton river on the evening of May 30th, 1842, where they pitched their tents and called it Fort Scott.

These troops consisted of Captain B. D. Moore, in command, Lieutenant William Eustis, Assistant Surgeon Dr. J. Simpson, and 120 enlisted men of companies A and C 1st U. S. Dragoons.

This command was soon after ordered on to Fort Leavenworth, and were replaced here by a part of the 1st Infantry. The officers with the infantry command were Major Graham, Captain Swords and Assistant Surgeon Dr. Mott.

Concluding the subject of the location of Fort Scott, Adjutant General L. C. Drum of the War Department, writes as follows:

"In reply to your letter of the 27th ultimo, addressed to the Secretary of War, asking certain information regarding the early settlement of Fort Scott, I have the honor to inform you that Fort Wayne, in the

Cherokee Nation, was abandoned on the 26th day of May, 1842, and companies A and C, 1st Dragoons, (which had formed its garrison) under the command of Captain B. D. Moore, 1st Dragoons, three officers and 120 enlisted men, marched to and occupied the new site which had been selected on the Marmaton river, twenty miles west of Little Osage Postoffice, on the 30th of May, 1842, to which they gave the name of Camp Scott, changed later to Fort Scott. The only other officers present with the command on that day were Dr. J. Simpson, Assistant Surgeon, and First Lieutenant William Eustis.

I have the honor to be Very Respectfully,
Your Ob't Serv't,
L. C. DRUM,
Adjutant General."

An army sutler came with the 1st Infantry named John A. Bugg, who, by virtue of his position, acted as postmaster.

COL. H. T. WILSON.

On the 13th of September, 1843, Hiero T. Wilson came up From Fort Gibson, where he had been located, and went into partnership with Mr. Bugg in the sutler business. They did business together until 1849, when Mr. Wilson bought out Mr. Bugg and he went to California. Mr. Wilson then became the sutler and U. S. Postmaster.

Col. Wilson, as he was always called, was born in Kentucky on the 6th day of September, 1806. He went to Fort Gibson as sutler of that post soon after it was established, and remained there about nine years, when he came to Fort Scott, as stated, in 1843. He lived here continuously from that time to the time of his death, August 6th, 1892. He was married to Elizabeth C. Hogan, on the 28th of September, 1847. They had three children, Virginia T., Elizabeth C. and Fannie W. Virginia, the eldest daughter, now Mrs. W. R. Robinson, was the first white child born in Fort Scott.

In Col. Wilson's residence in Fort Scott of nearly fifty years, he filled a prominent place in the political, social and commercial history of this part of the country. He saw the insignificant military station, and the wild and almost unknown surrounding country, with few bona fide white inhabitants nearer than a hundred miles, pass through all the panoramic changes from extreme frontier life to that of high civilization. For many years his only associates were the few army officers of the garrison; their days were passed with few incidents or recreations, and at night they went to sleep to the monotone howls of the prairie wolf.

After the Territory was organized Col. Wilson occupied many political positions, and although he was not what may be called active in politics, he was always consulted, and had great influence in the councils of his party. He was originally a Whig, and had great admiration for Clay and Webster, but after their day he associated himself with the Democratic party, and during the war was a strong Union Democrat. During the 60's he was very active in promoting the organization of the various railway companies forming to build roads into Southern Kansas, and active in his efforts to secure their construction to Fort Scott, which town

was always his pet and especial hobby. He was also
actively engaged in large mercantile affairs until 1868,
when he quit business. His life work was done. He
passed the remaining days of his ripe old age in the
peaceful calm of the home he had established so many
years ago.

SERGEANT JOHN HAMILTON.

Sergeant John Hamilton of the Ordnance Department of the army, came with the first troops, served
his term of enlistment and remained a resident of the
town and country until after the war. He superintended the construction of a good portion of the military
barracks, stables, etc., erected at Fort Scott in 1843
and 1844.

The military road from Fort Leavenworth was completed about 1843. The pike, or grade, like a railroad
grade, was constructed across all river and creek bottoms, and can still be seen across the Marias des Cygnes
bottoms south of the Trading Post, and also across the
Marmaton bottom at the Osbun farm northeast of Fort
Scott.

BARRACKS ERECTED.

In the year 1843 preparations were made for the construction of quarters for the officers and men, and the
necessary buildings for the quartermasters and commissary stores, ordnance supplies, etc. A saw mill was
erected about a mile up Mill Creek to be run by water
power. This mill gave the creek its name. A brick yard
was made near the mill. Then a detail of men from the

BARRACKS ERECTED.

infantry was kept busy making brick, and sawing lumber from the walnut, oak an ash logs cut from the surrounding timber on Mill Creek and Marmaton, which was very fine. Large trees, from one to four feet in diameter were plentiful. A square called the Parade Ground, now called the Plaza, was laid off, containing about two acres of ground. It was evidently intended that the points of this square should be due north and south, and east and west, but they miscalculated by a few degrees.

Around the northest side of the Plaza the buildings for the officer's quarters were erected. These consisted of four large double houses, 2½ stories high, with frame-timbers of oak twelve inches square, walnut siding and oak floors. The doors, door frames, lintels, windows, mantel-pieces, etc., were of two-inch walnut. The four blocks built for the officer's quarters are still standing, as good as ever. They were built in the uniform style of architecture which prevailed at all military posts at that time., and are very superior in construction. The most striking feature of these buildings is the broad porches extending along the entire front and also the rear of each, between the second and third floors, reached by broad flights of stairs at either end. The main roof projects and continues down over them from the attic story, and is supported by seven large doric columns fourteen feet in hight. These columns were made of solid walnut logs turned down into perfect shape and then bored through the center lengthwise to prevent checking or cracking when the columns seasoned.

On the other sides of the Plaza, were the buildings for quarters for the men, hospital, guard house, stables, etc., and in the center of the Plaza was an octagonal brick building for powder magazine. A well 90 or 100 feet deep was blasted down on the Plaza, which furnished a fair supply of water.

After all this work was completed the soldiers had but little to do, except an occasional scout, the guarding of supply trains, and their daily drill which took place *sure*, without fail, on all occasions and under all circumstances. The rest of the time until taps, they could play seven up, or perhaps straight poker. You may not quite understand what that extinct species of the game was. Well, they didn't *draw*. That was the Mississippi steamboat game you have heard so much about. It has been humed and will never, never be exhumed. But it was part of western life at that time, in the army, in the cabin on the prairie and in the "cabin" on the river.

RELICS OF A PAST ERA.

Those Government buildings erected fifty years ago stand to-day, and will stand indefinitely, as the relics and emblems of a past era. The mind can hardly conceive the vast changes which have taken place in this country during the half-century since they were erected. At this line of latitude the western limit of the United States was the Arkansas river instead of the Pacific ocean. The boundary line of the Nation was almost exactly 150 miles west of

Fort Scott. California, Utah, Arizona, New Mexico and Texas had not then been acquired. The country towards the setting sun west of the Missouri State line was called, in a general way, the "Indian Country." It was wild, desolate, silent, unknown. The people, even those living the nearest to it believed it to be a worthless barren plain, incapable of supporting a white population and fitted only for the home of Indians and wild animals. These had possession then, and it was presumed they would never be disturbed. An occasional pioneer might "'low it was gitten too much crowded" in his neighborhood, and move on a little further up the creek, but the idea of a general settlement of the country had not been considered. They concluded that the limit was about reached, and that the country was fringed with a frontier that would remain longer years than they took the trouble to think about.

But war was soon to send the volunteer soldiers trailing across it, enlightening them by actual contact, and through them the people, as to the great possibilities of this region as a habitable country. The boundary lines were to be adjusted and this country, instead of being on the very outer rim, was to become the geographical center of the Nation.

CHAPTER III.

ANNEXATION OF TEXAS—MEXICAN WAR.

THE year 1844 passed without much incident bearing directly or indirectly on the future of this section of the country. The Republic of Texas was not yet quite ripe but it was rapidly maturing and would soon be gathered into the Union, and add its grand empire to the territory of slavery. This occurred the next year—1845—and with the annexation came the war with Mexico. The annexation of Texas was the cause of the Mexican war. Texas claimed that its western boundary was the Rio Grande. Mexico claimed that it was the river Nueces. The United States "took the lawsuit with the property" and made it a pretext for a war which was essentially political and wholly unjustifiable. President Polk and his advisers saw in this war a prospect for still further acquisition of slave territory and the strengthening of the slave power. The acquisition of Texas had whetted the appetite of the Slave State men and the slavery propagandists; awakened the desire and renewed their determination to absolutely control the future of the United States. A mere equilibrium in territory and power between the North and South was not enough. They must have such a pronounced advantage that hereafter their wish would be the law, subject to no makeshift of a compromise. The north half of the Louisiana Purchase contained too many possibilities for free States, and the preponderance of territory must be gained now.

It is not the design to enter into the details of that war, but to catch the spirit which actuated the already powerful and rapidly increasing following of John C. Calhoun. It formed one of the converging lines which at that epoch were beginning to sweep through the Republic, dividing and materializing public thought and action, and leading up to and educating the people to a realization of an impending crisis.

One of the principal events of the war, however, which had a bearing on the future, was the winning by General Taylor of the battle of Buena Vista, by which he at once broke the back of the Mexican army and overthrew the Democratic party at home; for that battle made him—a Whig and a restrictionist—President of the United States, and put a curb, for a short time, on their high ambition. But the additional territory so much desired was gained by the acquisition of New Mexico, Arizona and Utah, for which, by the treaty of February 2, 1848, $15,000,000 was paid to Mexico.

WILMOT PROVISO.

During the war, Aug. 8, 1846, President Polk made an effort to stop it by a money proposition to Mexico.

He sent a message to Congress asking for an appropriation to pay for territory to be acquired. A bill was reported. David Wilmot, Hannibal Hamlin, Preston King and a few other Northern Democrats, who were not of those John Randolph called "Northern Doughfaces," held a caucus and decided among themselves that, inasmuch as Mexico had abolished slavery some twenty years before, all territory acquired from that country should come in free. Wilmot therefore offered the following proviso to the bill:

"*Provided*, That as an express and fundamental condition to the acquisition of any territory from the republic of Mexico by the United States, by virtue of any treaty that may be negotiated between them, and to the use by the Executive of the moneys herein appropriated, neither slavery nor involuntary servitude shall ever exist in any part of said territory, except for crime, whereof the party shall be first duly convicted."

This was the historic "Wilmot Proviso." The bill passed the House with this proviso, but was talked to death in the Senate and went over the session without a vote. And the two Whig generals, Scott and Taylor, went on with the war.

The Democratic party at that time contained no general officer of the army who was regarded as competent to conduct the war. A bill was introduced and passed one house authorizing the President to place Thomas H. Benton at the head of the army. But Benton had too many personal enemies in Congress and in the Cabinet, and the bill was finally defeated.

COMPROMISE OF 1850.

Congress in 1850 resumed its efforts to organize the country acquired from Mexico into Territories but without success. The whole matter was finally referred to a committee of which Henry Clay was chairman. The report of the committee formed the basis of a compromise—sometimes called the "Omnibus Bill"—the chief features of which were the admission of California as a free State, a territorial government for Utah and New Mexico, and prohibiting the slave-trade in the District of Columbia.

After a protracted discussion, a bill to organize Utah was passed, but the other measures of the bill went over to the next session, when they were brought forward separately and became laws, and the wrangle of 1850 was thus compromised. The effect was to allay the excitement that had so much agitated the country. The minds of the people were lulled to rest, and as 1851, '52 and '53 passed over without more than a slight increase in the boil and bubble of the political cauldron, it was hoped by all and believed by many that the slavery question was NOT irrepressible.

Outwardly, at least, all was quiet on the Potomac.

CHAPTER IV.

THE POST OF FORT SCOTT ABANDONED.

FORT SCOTT was garrisoned until April, 1853. The troops were then withdrawn, and the post practically abandoned. The buildings were left in charge of a sergeant, who, it is said, had instructions to permit their occupation by any respectable parties who would take care of them. At any rate, they were so occupied as fast as people came in. H. T. Wilson and John Hamilton and their families were at this time the only residents and constituted the entire population of Fort Scott. Colonel Wilson had the only store in this section of country. It was in a story and a half log house situated near what is now Market Square, about half way between the head of Main street and the lower part of National avenue. The few squatters within a radius of thirty miles or more came here to do their trading, if they had anything to trade. If they couldn't do any better, they would trade stories about happenings "back yonder in Kaintuckey" or "Injianny," or whatever haven of rest they may have come from.

SOME EARLY SETTLERS.

There were, of course, but few settlers up to the time

First Cabin Built on the Osage. 1844.

Post Sutler Store.

the Territory was opened for settlement in 1855. What few there were gravitated to the streams bordered with timber. They thought no claim was any account without a timber attachment.

It is impracticable to give the names of all of the earliest settlers, or anything of their biography. Several of them left before and some after the border troubles began; others before the war.

Among the very first settlers was Isaac N. Mills, who located on his farm near Marmaton in 1854. He was born in Kentucky in 1830.

W. R. Griffith also located near Marmaton in 1855. He came from Pennsylvania. He was the first Superintendent of Public Schools. He died at Topeka, February 12th, 1862.

Ephraim Kepley located on the Osage in 1854. He was born in North Carolina in 1825. He built the first cabin on the Osage river, in Bourbon county.

Robert Forbes and his brother David settled near Dayton in 1854, from Illinois.

D. T. Ralston, John Guttry, James Guttry, McCarty, Fly, Mitchell and Coyle located in what is now Marion township in 1855.

J. W. Wells came in 1855 from North Carolina.

Dr. J. R. Wasson, from Tennessee, located on the Osage in 1855.

Bryant Bangness settled on Drywood in 1855, from North Carolina. Wiley and Jacob Bolinger moved in on Mill Creek in 1855, from Missouri. Jacob Gross came in with the Bolingers and settled on Mill Creek in 1855.

William Hinton located on Osage in 1855, from Kentucky.

Dr. T. K. Julian, from Tennessee, first visited Fort Scott in 1854. Then he and his son T. B. Julian came back to Bourbon county and settled near Mapleton in 1855. T. B. Julian afterwards moved to Uniontown.

Joseph Oakley, from New York, settled on the Marmaton near Fort Scott in 1856. He died after the war.

Asa Ward moved in on Moore's Branch in 1856, from North Carolina.

Josiah Stewart located on Mill Creek in January, 1856. His sons, John J. and Amos came with him. John J. Stewart has always taken an active and prominent part in county affairs.

J. R. Anderson came to Bourbon county in 1856, and located near Xenia.

Thomas Osborne, with his sons Robert and James Osborne, moved here from Indiana and settled on the Osage in 1855.

John McNeil settled on the Osage in 1856. Pat Devereux in 1857. James and Timothy Hackett in 1857.

George W. Anderson and his son Jacob settled in Marion township in 1857.

I. N. Crouch went into Franklin township from Missouri. Joseph Oliver moved into Marmaton in 1857. J. R. Myrick located near Dayton in 1857. Joab Teague came in 1857 from North Carolina. Samuel Stevenson and sons, I. S. and S. A., in 1856.

M. E. Hudson, Wm. F. Stone, Adam Boyd, William Deeds, E. A. Roe, Wm. Baker, George Stockmyer,

Michael Bowers, Henry Bowers, E. P. Higby, Ed. Jones, D. R. Cobb, Ben. Workman, David Claypool, Walker, Huffman, Hathaway, Kelso, Atwood and the Endicotts were all early settlers, the most of them having settled in this county as early as 1855.

THE TIME FROM 1854 TO 1855.

Up to the year 1855 were the days of profound peace and quiet. The people enjoyed themselves after the manner of the frontier to the greatest extent. They all had good cabins, raised by the combined efforts of their neighbors, which at once became palaces of hospitality — that hospitality now almost obsolete. They had plenty to eat — game of all kinds — deer, wild turkeys, prairie chickens, fish from the streams, and their gardens and "patches" produced all else necessary.

As the manners and customs of frontier life are now things of the past, it may not be out of place to describe something of the mode of living among the pioneers up to the time the Territory was thrown open for settlement. To go into one of their cabins and take a meal with the family was a real satisfaction. The cooking was all done before immense fire-places. Cook stoves were not unknown, of course, but you would rarely see one. Their cooking utensils consisted of a big cast-iron skillet, with a cover made with a flange to hold live coals heaped on top, a tin coffee pot, possibly a bright tin reflecting oven, with legs, and one side open to be set near the fire to catch the heat, a big iron kettle and some smaller iron pots, a long-handled frying pan, iron spoons and knives and forks and some "tins." An ordinary water "bucket" was kept on a shelf in one corner, with a tin dipper or a gourd in it. Quite often they had instead of the bucket what many even quite old people of the present day have never seen. That is a "piggin." A piggin was made like a pail with one stave extending up about six inches with a rounded top for a handle.

Let us drop in on one of these families, say late in the fall of the year, and watch the wife get supper. First, a good fire is made with a back log, and plenty of oak and hickory wood on the andirons, which is allowed to burn down till there are plenty of coals. In the meantime a pot, hanging on the crane, containing the meat, is boiling. The skillet is placed on a bed of coals with coals heaped on the lid, and will soon be ready for baking the corn bread. In this instance it is corn bread and not dodger, the corn meal probably grated on a large hand grater, from new corn. It is made with eggs and shortening. Dodger and hoecake generally were mixed with eggs, venison gravy and milk also, but it was after supper. The meat is now taken from the pot, slashed across the rind, put in the reflector and baked brown. Big potatoes, sweet and Irish, are all this time lying in the hot ashes until their jackets are brown. The coffee pot is on, some "rashers" are cut from the "flitch" of bacon and the grease tried out; eggs are fried, and "dip" is made. Everything is timed to get done all at once, like the "wonderful one-horse shay." Now everything is placed on the white clothed table, together with dishes of cold meats, ves-

"COME TO SUPPER AND BRING CHEERS."

sels of rich yellow butter, cream, sweet milk, butter
milk and honey. Supper is now ready. If like some
now standing on the Osage, the cabin is a double one,
with a wide open porch between ; the men folks will
be in the "sitting room," and ten-year-old Jimmy will
be sent in, and will announce in a loud voice, "Come
to supper, and bring cheers." Each man totes in his
"cheer" and sits at the table. Probably the man of
the house, brought up in the church of Peter Cart-
wright, will ask a blessing. If so, it may be something
like this : "Kind Father, we thank Thee for Thy many
mercies. Bless these a-nourishments to our use. For-
give our sins. Protect us from evil. And in the end
save us, for Christ's sake." The words sounded like
simplicity itself. Heard from the lips of an Edwin
Booth, they would well up all the sweet idylic sentiments of Saint James.

Neighborship and hospitality were of the strong
tenets of the pioneer's character. All were welcome at
his house. No one was turned away hungry. Gold
and silver he had none, but such as he had he gave unto
all who came, the friend, the neighbor or the unknown
stranger.

He had but little communication with the "States."
He had no newspapers, and his library contained only
his old school books, Pilgrim's Progress and the Bible.
He knew but little of politics, but he could easily drive
center sixty yards, off hand, at the neighborhood shooting
match, where "first choice" was the hind quarter of a beef.
He heard more or less of the increasing and ominous
growls over the slavery question, but not until he sud-

denly found himself surrounded by vicious partisans from the contending sections, did he realize that his season of profound peace was over, that the harbinger of a storm had appeared, which was destined to stain the lintel of his cabin door with blood.

In these lame descriptions of our early settlers—squatters they were to all intents and purposes—an effort has been made to typify that class who kept to the extreme border of our frontiers, a people whose ancestors had steadily moved in westward front from the Atlantic through the "dark and bloody ground," a class then rapidly diminishing and who have now finally disappeared forever.

This seems necessary also, in order that one may realize all the conditions of a given period or situation, and to understand how the people lived in all respects.

THE CLIMATE.

The climate was another feature of those days. It was most delightful and enjoyable, especially in the fall of the year. It has changed in these later years, for civilization seems to have taken out the "wild taste." The atmosphere probably contained no more ozone than now, but it was wild ozone. It did not smell to heaven laden with iron filings and the abrasion of gold.

The immense prairies south and west—larger in extent than all western Europe—were annually burned over. The smoke from the autumn prairie fires permeated the entire atmosphere which came up to us from the grand pampas of the southwest toned down into superb Indian summer. But the wild prairies have disappeared beneath the plow, and Indian summer has disappeared with the Indian.

INDIAN SUMMER.

The beauty and grandeur of those autumn days can scarcely be described. One felt a lazy exhileration, and life here seemed the perfect ideal of existence on earth. The woods have unfurled a million banners, blended in all the colors of nature. The broad rolling prairies seemed as if formed by the stilled waves of a former and forgotten sea. The air, soft and dreamy, laden with the scent of wild flowers, went out to meet the coming day, whose rosy faced morn was ushered in by the songs of the mocking bird and the sweet chromatic cadence of the drumming grouse. And

> "The grey ey'd morn smiles on the frowning night,
> Checquering the eastern clouds with streaks of light."

The sun makes his daily circuit through a sea of smoky haze, until, hanging o'er the west like a huge illumined globe—shielded by the translucent rays of a glorious corona—he sinks below the horizon to the vesper song of the whipoorwill, and the gentle whisperings of the southwest wind.

CHAPTER V.

THE MILL OF THE GODS.

WE have now brought up the salient points of national history from the time when the United State acquired title to the domain lying west of the Mississippi river, insofar as they affect, directly or indirectly, the soon to be formed Territory of Kansas. We have noted especially the features affecting or bearing on the question of Slave Territory or Free Soil, and endeavored to mark out, like the "blaze" on trees through a forest for a new road, the many conflicting impulses which dominated the passions and prejudices of a great people.

It may be said that all this is unnecessary and uncalled for in the history of the local happenings of a single county. We do not think so. These local happenings, in fact the entire history of this county, was essentially and peculiarly political, brought about, controlled and "happened" as the resulting consequence of national politics. The history of counties in the old States might be written without so much extraneous detail. But those counties had no ancestors. They were progenitors. Bourbon County is their child. Its history cannot be truly and fairly written without going back to the base-line and bringing up the field notes.

The Louisiana Purchase was the base-line. The agitation of the slavery question began almost with that purchase. Slow at first, but gradually increasing, like the dread disease of consumption, until in the beginning of 1854, it had become the fevered and hectic topic of discussion in the Northern homestead and in the "big house on the lawn."

The National Legislature at that time was composed of the best minds of the country. The ward politician had not yet broken into Congress. The august Senate contained no resultant mouse from the parturition of local class sentiment, and no man of questionable personal honor had yet gained a seat. They were naturally and necessarily strong partisans; the men from the South were becoming bitterly so. There was an underlying feeling that the North was growing up to be the dominant power. They realized that, however distasteful, their candidate for the presidency must come from the North. Charles Sumner had enunciated the axiom, "Freedom is National; slavery is sectional;" the Northern press was using the license of printer's ink; the mud-sills were talking. All this angered them. Free speech and free press they no longer tolerated. They struck out, like a blinded rattlesnake, at every sound. Whom the gods would destroy they first make intolerant. Henceforth concessions were to be thrown to the winds; hereafter the policy was to be aggression. The Fugitive Slave Law was not enough. The Missouri Compromise—their own child, proposed by them, passed by them, and approved by President Monroe and his cabinet, of which John C. Calhoun was one—now stood in their road and must be swept away. The protesting hands of their Clays and Bentons were raised against such action, but were struck down by the spirit of Preston Brooks. The mills of the gods grind slow, but they grind exceeding fine.

Tools were necessary for the work in hand, and, like their Presidents, they also must come from the North.

KANSAS-NEBRASKA BILL.

On the 23rd of January, 1854, Stephen A. Douglas of Illinois, introduced a bill for the organization of the Territories of Kansas and Nebraska. This is known in history as the Kansas-Nebraska bill. The important features of the bill, affecting the Territory of Kansas, are copied from Sec. 32, and are as follows :

"That the constitution and all the laws of the United States which are not locally inapplicable, shall have the same force and effect within the said Territory of Kansas as elsewhere within the United States, except the eighth section of the Act preparatory to the admission of Missouri into the Union, approved March 6th, 1820, which, being inconsistent with the principle of non-intervention by Congress with slavery in the States and Territories, as recognized by the legislation of 1850, commonly called the compromise measures, is hereby declared inoperative and void; it being the true intent and meaning of this act not to legislate slavery into any Territory or State, nor to exclude it therefrom, but to leave the people thereof perfectly free to form and regulate their domestic institutions in their own way, subject only to the Constitution of the United States : *Provided*, That nothing herein contained shall be construed to revive and put in force any law or regulation which may have existed prior to the Act of the 6th of March, 1820, either protecting, establishing, prohibiting or abolishing slavery."

And on this Mr. Douglas addressed the Senate, outlining and advocating what he called the "great principles of squatter sovereignty, or non-intervention."

On the 3rd of March following, the Act passed the Senate by 37 to 14, and on May 22d it passed the House by 91 to 44, and President Pierce signed it on the 30th day of May.

The South had chosen her path. "Her feet go down to death; her steps take hold on hell." This was the high-water mark of the slave power. The solemn compact that had stood for thirty-four years was swept away like a "rope of sand." The converging lines of the irrepressible conflict were being drawn closer and closer until the culminating point was reached at Appomattox.

KANSAS TERRITORY ORGANIZED.

Kansas at last had a place on the map. It had been partly surveyed and the boundary lines designated and described. A governor and other Territorial officers were soon after appointed, and this experiment of non-intervention—this child of Squatter Sovereignty—was set adrift, to be buffeted, smitten, disgraced, in the confident hope that she would acquiesce in the demand of that force which instantly jumped at her throat, and quietly submit to be "sealed" to the South.

CHAPTER VI.

THE FIRST GOVERNOR.

A H. REEDER, the first Governor of Kansas Territory, arrived at Fort Leavenworth, and assumed the executive office October 7th, 1854. Soon after, with a party of other officials, he made a somewhat extended tour of observation through the eastern part of the Territory, and on his return that portion was divided into "Election Districts."

The district which included Fort Scott was denominated the Sixth District, and the metes and bounds were described as follows:

"Commencing on the Missouri State line, in Little Osage river; thence up the same to the line of the Reserve for the New York Indians, or the nearest point thereto; thence to and by the north line of said Reserve to the Neosho river, and up said river to and along the south branch thereof to the head; and thence by a due south line to the southern line of the Territory; thence by the southern and eastern line of said Territory to the place of beginning."

THE FIRST ELECTIONS.

On November 10th, Governor Reeder issued a proclamation for an election to be held in the Territory on the 29th day of November for the election of a Delegate to Congress. Fort Scott was designated as the place for holding the election for the Sixth District. The house of H. T. Wilson was named as the polling place, and the judges appointed were Thomas B. Arnett, H. T. Wilson and William Godfrey. J. W. Whitfield was the Pro-slavery candidate for Delegate, R. P. Finnekin, Independent, and John A. Wakefield Free State. In this district Whitfied received the entire vote cast, 105. Whitfield resided in Missouri at this time and made no pretense of being a citizen of the Territory.

On March 8, 1855, a proclamation was issued by Gov. Reeder, ordering an election for members of the Territorial Council and House of Representatives, to he held on Friday the 30th day of March, 1855. There were to be thirteen members of the Council and twenty-six Representatives, to constitute the "Legislative Assembly" of the Territory. The vote was to be by ballot. As there were yet no county or other municipal organizations, the election districts were provided for in the proclamation. The Sixth District remained the same as in the election of November 10, 1854. The place designated for holding the polls was the hospital building on the Plaza, and the judges of election appointed were James Ray, William Painter and William Godfrey. The proclamation also provided:

"That the Sixth Election District, containing two hundred and fifty-three votes, will constitute the Fifth Council District, and elect one member of the Council. Also, that the Sixth Election District shall be the Sixth Representative District and elect two members."

The result of this election was as follows: For Council Fifth District, William Barbee, 343 votes. For Representatives Sixth District, Joseph C. Anderson, 315, S. A. Williams 313, John Hamilton 36, William Margrave 16. And the returns being in due form and no protest filed, William Barbee for the Council, and Joseph C. Anderson and S. A. Williams for the House of Representatives, were by the Governor declared duly elected.

Nevertheless this election was grossly fraudulent, not only in this district, but in all others. It will be remembered that the district was nearly 50 by 100 miles square. William Barbee, mentioned above, had been appointed the January before to take the census of the district, and about March 1, thirty days before the election, filed his report giving the number of legal voters as 253. Many of these voters would have had to travel forty and fifty miles to the polling place. It is not reasonable to suppose that they took such a journey to vote. Most of the votes cast came from covered wagons camped on the Marmaton bottom, "for one day only," which Judge Margrave said, "just swarmed over from Missouri." But there was no protest in this district, and the men took their seats in the Legislature.

Barbee had no opposition. He and Anderson and Williams were voted for by the Pro-slavery men. Hamilton and Margrave received the feeble showing of the opposition.

William Barbee came here from Kentucky at the age of 29. He was a very fair man, and lived here several years. Barbee street in Fort Scott was named for him.

Joseph C. Anderson was never a resident of the district from first to last. He was the author of the "Black Laws" passed by this Legislature.

Samuel A. Williams was originally from Kentucky. He came here first in 1854, and afterwards brought his family, about six months before election, from Polk County, Missouri, driving an ox cart, containing his family, his chickens and two "cheers." He was no "voter." He had come to stay. He was a good man, a good citizen, and held many important positions. He died at his home in Fort Scott, August 13, 1873.

John Hamilton was "left over" from the regular army. He lived here in the town and in the county until after the war, as has been stated.

William Margrave was born in Missouri, February 17, 1818. He came here in the fall of 1854, and was appointed one of the first Justices of the Peace in the Territory, and the very first one appointed in this district. His commission bears date of December 5, 1854. He has lived here continuously ever since that time, and he is Justice of the Peace "'till yet." The Judge, in his quiet way, has always performed the duties of a good citizen, and always stood in the highest estimation in this community. Margrave street in the city of Fort Scott was named for him.

THE FIRST LEGISLATURE.

The first Legislature convened by order of the Governor at Pawnee, near Fort Riley, on the 2nd of July,

1855. Pawnee was 100 miles west of the Missouri State line at Westport. Governor Reeder said he took it out there to get it out of the way of political influence and to keep the legislators unspotted from the world. That was certainly the right idea and the right place if he could have made them stay there, but he couldn't do it. The statesmen said it was too dry, and too far from their base of supplies; and besides, as there were no houses in Pawnee, or in forty miles of it, they had to sleep in their wagons, or under them; and then again they had nothing to eat but jerked buffalo and Pawnee macaroni. This latter was a very succulent dish much sought after by the Pawnee Indians. It was made from the small entrails of antelope and fish-worms. The origin of this war-like tribe arose from this dish. Most any body would. The statesmen arose from it. Said they liked the legislature business all right enough but this wasn't an adjourned session of the Diet of Worms; they were not elected on that ticket. Said they didn't know what other Kansas Legislatures might do—no man in his right mind could tell, but as for their part they could not entertain such a diet, anyway, without something to go with it, and they didn't even have Bourbon County corn bread. Besides, they wanted to be nearer home where they could hear the honest coon-dog's deep-mouthed bay. So next morning they hitched up and drove down to Shawnee Mission, near Westport. That was as near home as they could get without going "plum over" into Missouri. Reeder could do nothing but set around and scratch his head and pawnee. He finally followed them down to Shawnee Mission. He told them they could not legally move, and could pass no valid laws if they did. They told him to be quiet or they would pass him—down the Missouri river on a raft. That made him madder than ever and he called them a lot of Border Ruffians. Then Stringfellow smote him hip and thigh, "and they wrote a letter unto the king," saying what a bad man this Reeder was, "and the king dismissed him with contumely." But the name give to them by Governor Reeder of Border Ruffian stuck to those fellows, and their kind, even to the third generation. Ainsi soit il.

THE BOGUS STATUTE.

The Legislature then went to work to pass laws for Kansas. It was now the 16th of July. By the 1st of September they had finished their labors which resulted in the preparation of an immense code of "laws," which have always been called and known as the "Bogus Statute of 1855." This Statute was called bogus principally because many of the members were not residents of the Territory, and they were themselves bogus; the elections were fraudulent in nearly every case, consequently their office was bogus. The sessions were held at Shawnee Mission against the will, order and veto of the Governor who had the only legal right to decide that point, as he claimed, consequently the whole business really had no legal status or right to be. But it was the prologue of the opening drama. The Pro-slavery men here showed their hand and the true spirit and intent of their party. They at once became blustering, arrogant, defiant and overbearing, and continually sought to pick quarrels with, and embroil every man into difficulties who opposed them. The few scattering and unorganized Free State men, in contemplation of such acts and such men, stood with raised and outstretched hands as if warding off a blow.

SAMPLE OF LEGISLATION.

The Legislature did more by its drastic, ill-tempered and senseless legislation to destroy the prospect of making Kansas a slave State than did all the Emigrant Aid Societies, John Brown and other Northern fanatics put together. As a sample of their legislation and to show the spirit which controlled the Pro-slavery side on the threshold of the struggle, the following section of their laws is quoted:

"SEC. 12. If any person, by speaking or by writing, assert or maintain that persons have not the right to hold slaves in the Territory, or shall introduce into Kansas, print, publish, write, circulate, or cause to be introduced into the Territory, any book, paper, magazine, pamphlet or circular containing any denial of the rights of persons to hold slaves in this Territory, such person shall be deemed guilty of a felony, and punished by imprisonment at hard labor for a term not less than two years."

This made it a penitentiary offense for a person to take a Free-State paper, or to argue the question with a neighbor, even at his own fireside. The present generation cannot conceive that a body of educated and intelligent American men could have seriously placed such a law, and a hundred of similar tenor and import on the statute books of a State. But the indescribable fanaticism on the question of human slavery had made them, as a people, just that intolerant.

On the other hand the Northern people, as a people, said to the South exactly this: We have made a constant, consistent and honest effort to restrict slavery to its present limits, and although the sacred compact which has stood for a third of a century is broken down, let us peacefully abide the provisions of the squatter sovereign principle. And we now say to you Southern people, and you may be fully assured that, although we shall not desist from those open, honest efforts which we have constantly made for restriction and which efforts will be vigorously continued to make Kansas a Free State, we shall neither openly or secretly resort to any measures which can tend to disturb the tranquillity of the slave States, or thereby to affect the prosperity of the Nation. And thus at the commencement of that most momentous era was the virgin Territory of Kansas handed over to those two contending sections, who had "come to ope the purple testament of bleeding war."

It looked dark for the side of Freedom. Its enemies controlled the Administration; they controlled all the branches of the Territorial Government and they controlled the front door through which emigration must enter.

GOVERNMENT BUILDINGS SOLD.

The buildings erected and the improvements made by the Government at Fort Scott were estimated to have cost $200,000. They were sold at public auction on the 16th day of May, 1855, by Major Howe, Assistant Quartermaster of the U. S. Army, for less than $5,000 for the whole business. The officers quarters— the four principal blocks of buildings, were disposed of as follows: A. Hornbeck bought the first block, on the west corner of the Plaza for $500. H. T. Wilson the next for $300, E. Greenwood the next for $505, and J. Mitchell bought the next building on the east for $450. The other buildings were sold to different parties for nominal sums. Of course, this not being a Government Reservation, the title to the land on which these buildings stood did not pass by this transaction, and it was so understood by the purchasers. But they concluded to "let the hide go with the tallow," and take their chances of acquiring title either from the Government as pre-emptors, or, that some time in the future when the town shall have been surveyed and platted, and a legally incorporated town company organized, they could obtain deeds. This plan was agreed on and was afterwards carried out.

CHAPTER VII.

BOURBON COUNTY ORGANIZED.

THE County of Bourbon was organized, together with thirty-two other counties by the act of the Bogus Legislature contained in Chapter 30, of the Bogus Statutes. This Act or Chapter of that code was acted on and passed by the Legislature at the session held at Shawnee Mission, early in August, 1855, to take effect from and after the date of passage, although the statutes were not compiled or completed and published until, probably, October 25th of that year.

In Section 4 of said Chapter 30, the boundary lines of Bourbon County were fixed and described as follows:

"Beginning at the southeast corner of Linn county; thence south thirty miles; thence west twenty-four miles; thence north thirty miles; thence east twenty-four miles to the place of beginning."

These descriptions are very nearly correct, except that the first sectional line is not quite parallel with the Missouri State line, and the border sections along that line are fractional, and there is a jog in the range line on the west side of the county.

The Legislature, at the request of William Barbee

and S. A. Williams, who were both originally from old Kentucky, named this county "Bourbon"—especial brand not given. They thought, like the old boys used to say: "Some is better than others, but it's all good." So they gave it a good send off by giving it a good name.

McGee county was named for old Milt McGee who was then a member of the Legislature, "from Westport, Missouri." Everybody knew old Milt way up to the 60's.

Anderson county was named for one of our first Representatives, Joseph C. Anderson.

Wilson county was named for Col. H. T. Wilson, of Fort Scott.

Bourbon County retained its original territory until by act of the Legislature, approved February 13, 1867, entitled, "An Act to define the boundaries of Bourbon, Crawford and Cherokee counties," the boundaries of Bourbon County were defined and described as follows:

"SEC. 1. That the boundary of Bourbon County shall commence at the southeast corner of the county of Linn; thence run south, on the east line of the State of Kansas to the southeast corner of section (24) twenty-four, township (27) twenty-seven, range (25) twenty-five; thence west to the southwest corner of section (23) twenty-three, township (27) twenty-seven, range (21) twenty-one; thence north to the southwest corner of Linn county; thence east to the place of beginning."

By this act the county was cut down to about twenty-five miles square.

In the Government survey of this State the base line, or beginning line, for townships of six miles each was made the north line of the State, and townships were numbered from number one on down southward; and the range lines, also six miles apart, were numbered east and west from the sixth principal meridian, or guide meridian, which is near the city of Wichita.

Bourbon County contains 407,680 acres of land. The contour of the face of the country is high, rolling prairie, with a general slope from west to east, the general direction of all the larger streams being from west to east, in common with the entire State. The west line of the State has an altitude of between 2,000 and 3,000 feet. At the sixth principal meridian the altitude is about 1,000 feet. At the east line of Bourbon County it is 650 feet.

The county is very well watered. The more considerable streams being the Osage river on the north and through the northern tier of townships, Mill creek and Marmaton river through the central portion, and Pawnee and Drywood creeks in the southern part. There is the usual amount of bottom land along these streams, which are, of course, very rich, but these lands are not especially desirable over those of the high prairie for farming purposes, for the reason that they are colder and harder to get into to work during a wet spring and do not stand a dry time later in the season much better than the high prairie, besides the high lands are, as far as the soil is concerned, rich enough except on some quarter sections scattered throughout the county on which the stone is too near the surface. The soil of the prairie lands is, generally speaking, of a limestone formation and richer of itself than a sandstone formation. Under the black soil is about eighteen inches of a dark brown sub-soil, then a stratum of three to eight feet of yellow clay, then two to four feet of shale or slate stone. Under that in a good portion of the county is a layer of hard bituminous coal from eight to twenty inches. This is especially true of the east half of the county. Under all this is a solid stratum of pure limestone from four to six feet in thickness, then comes a stratum of from sixteen to thirty feet of soapstone. Under that, on a limestone bedrock, water is generally obtained. These strata vary, however—and in fact the entire geological formation changes in certain sections of the country. About the central part of the county there are sections which are pure sandstone formation, which contains an almost inexhaustible supply of the very best quality of sandstone flagging. Limestone for the manufacture of lime, and for building stone is easily obtained in any part of the county. In Fort Scott, and the neighborhood, is found extensive quarries of cement rock, which produces the best grade of hydraulic cement.

THE FIRST COUNTY OFFICERS.

The Secretary of the Territory and Acting Governor Daniel Woodson, appointed a part of the first officers of Bourbon County, after its organization, on the 31st day of August, 1855, as follows: Samuel A. Williams, Probate Judge, H. T. Wilson and Charles B. Wingfield County Commissioners, and B. F. Hill, Sheriff. And on the 22d of September, Governor Wilson Shannon appointed J. J. Farley clerk of the Board of County Commissioners, or County Clerk, as we call it now, and John F. Cottrell, Constable, and Thomas Watkins Justice of the Peace for Bourbon County.

On the 9th of November commissions were issued to Wiley Patterson, Cowan Mitchell, Henry Miller and D. Guthrie, as Justices of the Peace. J. J. Farley, County Clerk, was appointed Register of Deeds.

Fort Scott was about this time designated as the County Seat.

In November, 1855, the Board of County Commissioners met and divided the county into townships, as follows: Little Osage, Timberhill, Russell, Scott and Drywood. The townships as they now exist are, Osage, Freedom, Timberhill and Franklin on the north, Scott, Marmaton, Mill Creek and Marion through the center, and Drywood, Pawnee and Walnut on the south.

About the close of the year 1855, B. F. Thompson and Branham Hill were appointed Justices of the Peace, Alexander Howard and William Moffatt, constables, and H. R. Kelso, coroner, in and for Bourbon County.

THE NEUTRAL LANDS IN BOURBON COUNTY.

The county of McGee, organized at the same time as Bourbon, included what is now Crawford and Cherokee counties, and was all Cherokee Neutral Land. A six mile strip off the south side of Bourbon county, between townships 26 and 27, and between ranges 21 and 25, was also in the Cherokee Neutral Land. This strip is more exactly described as follows:

The south ⅓ of Township 26, of Ranges 22, 23, 24, 25. The east part of south ⅓ Township 26 of Range 21. The north ⅔ of Township 27 of Ranges 22, 23, 24, 25. The east part of ⅔ of Township 27 Range 21.

As will be seen hereinafter, a good part of these lands were squatted on by settlers in direct violation of treaty stipulations with the Cherokee Indians. In many cases, however, the squatters were innocent of any intention to trespass.

FORT SCOTT INCORPORATED AS A TOWN.

Fort Scott was incorporated as a town by Chapter 40 of the Bogus Statutes, which chapter was acted on and passed by the Legislature on the 30th of August, 1855.

Section 1 of that chapter provides that the land set forth and defined in the plat of said town shall be incorporated into a town by the name of Fort Scott.

Section 4 provides that "the first Board of Trustees of the town of Fort Scott shall consist of H. T. Wilson, A. Hornbeck, Thomas Dodge, R. G. Roberts, F. Demint and Thomas B. Arnett."

Section 8 provides that the trustees shall have power to collect taxes, regulate dramshops, to restrain and prevent the meeting of slaves, etc.

But little is now known about some of the trustees. A. Hornbeck was a merchant. He came in from Missouri, and went back there after two or three years' residence here. Dodge was an Indian trader, and had been all his life. Thomas B. Arnett opened and kept the first hotel ever in Bourbon county. It was in the house on the west corner of the Plaza, known afterwards as the Fort Scott, or Free State Hotel. He fell dead one Sunday, sometime afterwards, while attending religious services in the Government Hospital building, probably because, as town trustee, he had not been strict enough in "regulating dramshops."

MORE ELECTIONS.

On the 1st of October, 1855, an election was held under provisions of the Legislature, for Delegate to Congress. J. W. Whitfield was again the Pro-slavery candidate, and received 242 votes in this county.

There was no Free State candidate, and the Free State men took no part in this election.

A convention had been called at Topeka on the 19th day of September, to take measures to form a State Constitution. An election was held for Delegates to the Topeka Constitutional Convention, on the 9th of October. A. H. Reeder was also voted for by the Free State men for Delegate to Congress. The town of Fort Scott cast 27 votes. There appears to be no record of a county vote.

The Convention met at Topeka on the 23d day of October. A Free State Constitution was framed, and an election for its adoption held on the 15th day of December. Again there is no record from Bourbon County. The fact of the matter is, there were but few Free State men in this county at that time. There were not enough of them to form anything like an organization, or even a circulating chain of intelligence among themselves. Each one was isolated from his kind, and lived like a rabbit in a burrough. He kept his eyes and ears open, but he kept his mouth shut. There were less than 300 legal votes in the entire county, and not more than thirty of these were Free State men. The first immigration into this county was largely from the Southern States. The territory lay adjacent to a slave State, and it was natural that it should assimilate with the peculiar institution of the South. Further north, where the parties were more nearly equal in number, the Free State men went to the polls; they protested, however vainly, against the fraudulent elections; they took concerted action for self-defense. Here they could do neither. As yet they were in too great a minority. They could only sit down and wait; wait to see how far and to what extent the Northern people would go to meet the open defiance of the maddened and blinded partisans of ultra pro-slaveryism; wait for immigration to reach down this far and give them help. It seemed now to them like a losing contest. The migratory hordes of the Pro-slavery party had, under the faint pretense of "election," taken possession of the Territory, driven out the first Governor—an able, fair and just man—and published to the world their statute of "laws," which hung over the Territory for five years like the web of a mammoth spider.

THE SECOND GOVERNOR.

Wilson Shannon of Ohio, was appointed to succeed Governor Reeder. He arrived at Shawnee Mission and assumed the duties of his office on the 7th of September, 1855, a few days after the adjournment of the Bogus Legislature.

Governor Shannon had nothing to do with the election of March 30th, 1855, and was, of course, in no way responsible for the action of either faction; and, although surrounded exclusively by Pro-slavery men, bravely endeavored, during his short administration, to do his duty as he saw it.

POLITICAL ATMOSPHERE OF BOURBON COUNTY.

The situation of Bourbon County during the years 1855, 1856 and 1857 was peculiar. It was different from that of any other county or portion of the Territory. The county was away down in the southeast, isolated, and as yet out of the line and track of immigration, and as yet out of the way of the partisan troubles which held full sway in the country further north. There were some men—their number could be counted on your fingers—drifted in during these years, who hung around here more or less, who were of the very worst class; border ruffians themselves, and leaders above all others of that ultra, uncompromising Pro-slavery element whose politics was simply extermination —extermination of Free State sentiment—extermination of Free State men, if that were necessary. These were men like Dr. Hamilton, Captain G. A. Hamilton, Alvin Hamilton, W. B. Brockett, G. W. Jones, G. W. Clark. E. Greenwood, Sheriff Ben Hill and others. But few of these made any pretense to citizenship, but made Fort Scott one of their many stopping places or headquarters. Their followers—their "men"—were of that class they, themselves, called "poor white trash." They were never able to own a slave and never expected to be. They were that grade of men who saw everything through the diseased perceptions of an incomplete nature and a smothered intelligence. The men from the South who came here as bona fide settlers to make homes for themselves and families were of a different grade. They were Pro-slavery, and desired as a political question, that Kansas should come into the Union as a slave State. They were thoroughly imbued with the principles of Squatter Sovereignty, but had no more idea or design of a criminal crusade in order to accomplish their political ends than did Stephen A. Douglas himself. They staid here law abiding men during this first war; they staid here good Union men during the Union war, and lived and died among us under the flag of Clay and Benton, either the one or the other of whom had been their household god since the days of their youth.

As for the Northern men, a few of whom were now finding their way into this county, they, also, were in some sense different from their brethren further north. They came without "aid" or other influence, except the desire to build up a home. They came very generally from Pennsylvania, Ohio, Indiana and Illinois. They were Free State men and finally voted for a Free State Constitution. But they were not anti-slavery in the sense of being Abolitionists. They did not want slavery; they did not want free negroes; they simply did not want any "nigger" at all. Many of them were Democrats; many were Republicans; but they had no desire to interfere with the "peculiar institution" of the South further than to keep it out of Kansas. They came here to make Kansas a State and to make it free.

It is not within the scope and design of this work to detail the historical incidents and the public acts of historical men or notorious characters outside of Bourbon County, except insofar as they concern or affect, directly or indirectly our own local history. So far, an attempt has been made to keep in touch with the prominent men of those times, the animus of political parties and the social bias of the contending forces.

It may be possible that the accurate and complete history of our State can only be thus prepared, block by block, and the checquered and mosaic tablet be handed down to the future as the "History of Kansas."

CHAPTER VIII.

TONE OF PRO-SLAVERY PAPERS

THE year 1856 opened in the northeastern part of the Territory and along the Kaw valley, in turmoil, violence and murder. Armed factions were almost daily coming into the conflict. The Free State men were being armed and drilled for defense. The Pro-slavery men were being reinforced from South Carolina, Alabama and the entire South, for the openly declared purpose of overawing the Free State men by violence and murder.

One sample of the tone of their newspapers at that time is here given. The Kickapoo Pioneer, in speaking of Free State immigrants, said:

"It is this class of men that have congregated at Lawrence, and it is this class of men that Kansas must get rid of. And we know of no better method * * * than to meet in Kansas and kill off this God-forsaken class of humanity as soon as they place their feet upon our soil."

Bourbon County had as yet but little of this disorder and violence. But the disturbing elements were to come in very soon, and peace bid farewell for many years.

THE TOPEKA CONSTITUTION.

The first political move of the year 1856 was the election of officers under the Topeka Constitution, which took place January 15. Charles Robinson was the leading candidate for Governor, and M. W. Delahay for Congress. W. R. Griffith of Bourbon County, was voted for as State Auditor, but received less votes than G. A. Cutler for that office. Griffith was also a member of this Constitutional Convention.

The Topeka Constitution was not recognized by Congress. The Legislature elected under it never had any practical existence, nor was it expected to have, or probably, intended to have. The conventions of August 14 and September 15; the elections of October 9, December 15 and January 15, the Constitutional Convention and the Topeka Constitution, were intended by the Free-State leaders to serve—like toys given to impatient children—to occupy the minds of our Free-State men; to solidify the growing "Anti-Pro-slavery" elements of all shades in the North, and by publishing to the world their platforms, resolutions and constitutions, to furnish educating exponents of the principles, policy and design of the Free-State party.

As was expected, some of the ultra Abolitionists were dissatisfied. The word "white" was not eliminated from the new Constitution; its tone was for peaceful solution, instead of for the aggravation of conflict as they desired. They kicked over the traces, but they were simply "cut out" and driven away.

The Free-State leaders at this time—among them

Charles Robinson, A. H. Reeder, M. J. Parrott, Joel K. Goodin, M. W. Delahay—were strong men. The Convention and the Legislature elected under it were composed of good and true men. They raised here the first signal light of Freedom, against which were already breaking the black, seething waves of disunion.

TROUBLE COMMENCES.

The first invasion into Bourbon County by the Pro-slavery men occurred in the spring of 1856. A party of about thirty South Carolinians, headed by G. W. Jones, came in and stopped temporarily in Fort Scott. Under pretense of looking for homes, these men visited most of the settlers in the county, ascertained where they were from and their politics, what property they had, and their means of defense, and made a complete list of all the Free-State men. Then, later in the season, about July, the Free-State men were again visited, and were told they must leave the Territory. A system of espionage, intimidation and arrest was commenced. Their stock was driven off; their cabins fired into in the dead of night, and they were often taken under pretended arrest to Fort Scott, where they would be advised that it was a much healthier country further north for their class. The object was to so harass and intimidate them that they would leave their claims and such property as could not be easily moved, and get out of the Territory, which the Pro-slavery people had decided was their own by right, not of discovery, but "non-intervention," and "Squatter

Sovereignty." The matter was actually presented to
the masses of the South in the light that, as the re-
strictive compromise law had been wiped out, this was
slave territory; Free-State men were interlopers, and
had no more rights here than they had in South Carolina. A Free-State man would not be allowed to live
in South Carolina; why should he be here?

Anyway, their plans worked well. The Free-State
men were not strong enough then for resistance or
defense, and most of them left. This was in execution
of the concerted plans of Major Buford and his lieutenant, G. W. Jones, who had arrived on the 7th of
April, at Westport, Missouri, with a large body of
armed men, some three hundred in number, from Alabama, Georgia and South Carolina. Buford was a kind
of brigadier general in the army of invasion, and had
charge of the border, with the instructions, among
others, to search all steamboats coming up the Missouri
river, for Free-State passengers, and all emigrant wagons coming from the East and North.

TEXAS RANGERS—EXPEDITION TO MIDDLE CREEK.

Late in the summer of this year a squad of fellows
came into Bourbon County from the south, who called
themselves "Texas Rangers." They were all well
armed and mounted, and wore spurs as big as a tin
plate. Their saddles were of the regulation Texas
pattern, with immense saddle blankets, with the "Lone
Star" worked in the corner.

Altogether, they were a very "fierce and warlike

people," and wanted to go right into the business immediately. So, after laying around town two or three days whetting up their bowie knives and running bullets they got some of G. W. Jones' South Carolinians, added a few of the fellows who lived in Fort Scott, and away they went, headed for Osawatomie, to rout out John Brown. The company was under command of Wm. Barnes, G. W. Jones and Jesse Davis. They got up as far as Middle Creek in Linn County where, about August 25th, they were met by Captains Shore and Anderson with a company of Free State men of about the same number. After a lively skirmish, in which three or four volleys were exchanged, they let go and skedaddled back to Fort Scott, pushing on their bridle-reins and with saddle-blankets flying. They had such big stories to tell about being closely pursued by 2,000 yankees, who would soon be on them to burn and murder, that everybody in town, men, women and children, dogs and niggers, took to the woods and laid out all night. It is said the Texas Rangers never stopped till they got back to Red River. Geo. W. Jones buried himself in the wilds of Buck Run.

One of the recruits from Fort Scott on this expedition was a man named Kline, who had just started a newspaper which he called the "Southern Kansan." He had issued only two numbers of it when he felt a call to help "advance the banner of the holy crusade." He laid down the "shooting stick" to take up the shooting iron. But it was an unlucky exchange, for, at the first fire of "leads," the "devil" fired him into the "hell-box," and he remained in "pi" forever.

This was the only report in the "remark" column of their muster-roll.

THE TOPEKA LEGISLATURE.

The Legislature elected under the Topeka Constitution met first on the 4th of March, and adjourned to meet at Topeka on the 4th of July, 1856. At that date they assembled and attempted to open a session, but they were met by Col. Sumner of the regular army, who ordered them to disperse.

SHANNON RESIGNS—GEARY APPOINTED.

Governor Wilson Shannon, who had now been in office several months, became distasteful to the Administration and the Pro-slavery party, and retired from office on the 21st of August, 1856.

Secretary Woodson, an implement of the Pro-slavery people, became acting Governor until John W. Geary of Pennsylvania, was appointed, and assumed the office in September following.

TERRITORIAL LEGISLATORS FOR BOURBON COUNTY.

On October 6th, 1856, an election was held for members of the second Territorial Legislature, which was to meet the following January. In this county there were to be two members elected. There were three candidates in the field, who received votes as follows: B. Brantly, 176 votes; W. W. Spratt, 127 votes; R. G.

Roberts, 60 votes. Brantley and Spratt were declared elected.

These men were Pro-slavery. The Free State men had nearly all been driven out, as has been stated, and what few were left had neither disposition or opportunity to vote. The Pro-slavery people also voted at this election for J. W. Whitfield for Delegate to Congress, and voted for calling a Constitutional Convention.

The closing hour of 1856 was the darkest hour for freedom in Kansas. Its closing day marked the first year of the preliminary struggle of the civil war. The lines were being drawn and public sentiment solidified throughout the Nation by the co-efficients of intolerance, prejudice and hate.

CHAPTER IX.

BOURBON COUNTY OFFICIALS.

THE county officers at the beginning of 1857 remained about as they had been in 1856. A. Hornbeck was County Treasurer. The same Board of County Commissioners, and B. F. Hill was still Sheriff. The full representation in the Legislature was: Blake Little in the Council, W. W. Spratt and B. Brantley in the House. Blake Little had been elected to succeed William Barbee, who died sometime before. Mr. Little was quite an old man, and always regarded as a good citizen. He was Pro-slavery in politics. His son John H. and daughter Mary were living at Fort Scott with him. He left here in 1859 and went to Arkadelphia, Arkansas.

NEW TOWNS.

The second session of the Territorial Legislature was convened at Lecompton on the 12th of January. Among the laws passed was an act incorporating the town of Sprattsville in Bourbon County, an act establishing a State road from Barnesville to Cofachique. Sprattsville was near where Dayton now is. It never advanced in "growth and population" further than the survey stakes for corner lots. It perished. It was located by W. W. Spratt, who was that year in the Legislature.

The dense population in this connty at that time seemed to require the "building up" of more towns. Already foundations for future cities were being laid, which in the near future were to become "busy marts of trade," "manufacturing and railroad centers;" have the machine shops and vote bonds, and have a macadam tax, and a cracker factory. The probable location of the depot was another question of vast moment. It must not be so located that it would draw business to one point of the town at the expense of another. That must be guarded against. Everyone with a piece of land suitable for an "addition" said he would guard against it if it took half the land he had.

All these things were within the vision of the founders, although the nearest railroad was yet two hundred miles away.

MAPLETON LOCATED.

Mapleton was first located in May, 1857. The Town Company were J. C. Burnett, E. P. Higby, Mr. Morton, B. B. Newton, S. W. Cheever and D. Scott. This Company soon afterwards abandoned the town project and was dissolved.

Afterwards a new Company was organized by Wm. Baker, Dr. S. O. Himoe, A. Wilson, John Hawk, James Huffnagle and M. E. Hudson. This Company first called the town Eldora, but after a time the name was changed back to Mapleton. Dr. S. O. Himoe was appointed the first Postmaster on October 15th, 1857. E. P. Higby was appointed early in 1858 and continued the Postmaster for more than thirty years. E. Greenfield established the first store in 1858.

Mapleton has always been a prominent place in this county. It is located in the beautiful valley of the Osage, surrounded by an agricultural country unsurpassed, and a thrifty, intelligent people.

RAYVILLE.

Rayville, of which considerable will be said hereafter, was located by the two Ray brothers. It was on the Osage, about half way between the points now known as Ft. Lincoln and Mapleton. Rayville never became a great manufacturing center, either; but they manufactured some Bourbon County history there. It had at one time a store and a postoffice. But it finally perished, also, and was laid "under the sod and the dew" by the side of Sprattsville. It was too near Mapleton.

MEANS OF COMMUNICATION.

The means the people of Bourbon County then had for mail facilities and communication with the outside world were decidedly limited. They had a stage line established between Fort Scott and Jefferson City, Mo., and the stage, an old bob-tailed "jerky," such as is now to be seen only in "Wild West shows," made the trip once a week; that is, when the creeks were not up and there was no other preventing providence. This line brought in the Eastern mail, and its arrival and departure were important events. Col. Arnett was the local agent, and he conducted the business with characteristic flourish. Three times a week they had a horseback mail from Westpoint, Montevallo and Sarcoxie, Mo., Baxter Springs, Osage Mission and Cofachique. These radiating lines indicated the importance already attached to Fort Scott as a distributing point. All freight came on ox-wagons from Kansas City, Mo., down the old military road.

There were then but three saw mills in the county: one on the Little Osage, near the future site of Fort Lincoln; one on the same stream above Sprattsville, and one on the Marmaton six miles west of Fort Scott. There was an abundant growth of black walnut, sycamore, cottonwood, oak, coffee bean, linn, etc., along the Little Osage, Mill Creek, Marmaton and Drywood.

GOOD BASS FISHING ON MILL CREEK.

CHAPTER X.

MORE POLITICS.

THE Territorial Legislature in February, 1857, passed an act dividing the Territory into three judicial districts. The first step in the Lecompton Constitution movement was taken February 19th by the Legislature passing an act providing for the election of delegates to a convention to frame a State Constitution. The act provided for a census to be taken, on the basis of which the Governor was to apportion among the precincts the sixty delegates to the Convention. The delegates were to be elected on the second Monday in June, which was the 15th, and were to meet at Lecompton on the first Monday in September. Governor Geary vetoed the bill, but the Legislature passed it over the veto, by a nearly unanimous vote.

On the 4th of March, 1857, James Buchanan became President.

In his Inaugural Address he said:

"Congress is neither to legislate slavery into any Territory or State, nor to exclude it therefrom, but to leave the people thereof perfectly free to form and conduct their own domestic institutions in their own way. As a natural consequence, Congress has also prescribed, that when the Territory of Kansas shall be admitted as a State, it shall be received into the Union with or without slavery, as the Constitution may prescribe at the time of admission. A difference of opinion has arisen in regard to the time when the people of a Territory shall decide this question for themselves. This is happily a matter of but little importance, and besides it is a judicial question, which legitimately belongs to the Supreme Court of the United States, before whom it is now pending and will, it is understood, be speedily and finally settled."

Two days afterward the Supreme Court handed down the decision in the Dred Scott case. The gist of that decision is this: The Missouri Compromise, so far as it excluded slavery from the Louisiana Purchase, north of 36.30° was unconstitutional; that Congress had no power to prohibit slavery from any portion of the Federal territory, nor to authorize the inhabitants thereof to do so; that negroes are not citizens, and have no rights as such. Or, in other words, that Kansas was de jure Slave Territory, as it was de facto.

"Jeems" evidently knew on the 4th of March what that decision was to be as well as he did on the 6th.

SLAVES IN BOURBON COUNTY.

At this time there were in Fort Scott and Bourbon County about thirty negro slaves, owned by various families from the slave States. They were legally held as such under the Dred Scott decision. Kansas was slave Territory.

Slaves were bought and sold in this county as late as

August, 1857. The records of the county show that Wiley Patterson purchased a negro woman slave of James M. Rucker for $500.00 at that date.

GOV. GEARY RESIGNS—GOV. WALKER APPOINTED.

Early in March, 1857, Governor Geary sent his resignation in a letter to St. Louis, the nearest telegraph station, to be telegraphed from there to Washington. He followed it himself soon after, and left the Territory somewhat hastily.

> "He tuck his hat and lef' very sudden
> Like he gwine to run away,"

Geary was a good man. He took office a Pro-slavery man, but he misunderstood what the Administration and the leading Pro-slavery men in Kansas wanted. He based his policy on the principles of justice and the protection of all persons in their rights. That was not what they wanted. They were also mistaken in their man, and by denying him of all means of self-protection in the matter of troops, etc., and by personal assault and attempts at assassination, they finally drove him from the Territory.

The Administration then concluded to put in a Southern man for Governor, and Robert J. Walker was appointed on the 26th of March. Walker, it is true, was born in Pennsylvania, but he had spent the years of his manhood in Mississippi. F. P. Stanton was appointed Secretary and came first, in April, and took charge as Acting Governor.

MORE IMMIGRANTS.

Bourbon County had now began to attract more attention and become better known to the people of the East and North. The few settlers who had found their way down here "writ back." While their letters did not bear any very encouraging word about the state of political affairs or the peaceful condition of the people, they did tell of a beautiful country, genial skies, a spring that opened in March instead of May, and an opportunity for getting land enough so that "John" and "Mary" could both have a farm when they "come of age."

Fort Scott had also become one of the noted points in the new Territory, and many young men were attracted here to make this the starting point for their future. A few who came were unfitted for the life of pioneers. They generally came from the cities, and as much on what they called a tour of adventure as anything. But they found that even at the best hotel the bed consisted of a straw tick and a buffalo robe, the bath room was the Marmaton, and the means of washing the face and hands were at the bottom of the back stairs in a tin basin with hard water and soft soap. They might have withstood all these luxuries, but when they came to the dinner table that jarred 'em loose. The "menu" consisted of cornbread, bacon, fried potatoes and corn coffee with "long sweetnin'. After wrestling with those delicacies for a short time they would generally conclude they had seen enough of the "border troubles" and skip back home fully determined to "go with their States" and let Kansas go Free Trade and Woman's Rights if it wanted to, or go to any other place, they were going home where they could get some of "mother's cooking."

During the fall of 1856 and the winter and spring of 1857, there were also coming in from the slave States— aside from the followers of Buford—a large contingent of men, who were good citizens where they came from, and remained here to the end, good citizens and good men. The country knew none better.

Biographies and biographical sketches of the old settlers cannot be given in this volume. Their biographies would furnish material for a much larger book than this. It may some day be prepared. An attempt will be made in this book to give a slight sketch or mention only of the more prominent men who took hold of the throttle valve and helped turn on steam.

Among those who came in this spring were the following:

Dr. John H. Couch, with his family, arrived May 30, 1857. Dr. Couch was born in Lexington, Kentucky, April 8, 1827. He obtained a fine collegiate and medcal education in that State, and went from there to Monroe, Wisconsin, where he married Miss Lillis Andrick. He was a strong Democrat and never hesitated to vigorously denounce what he thought wrong in his party, or any other. His heart was big. Many and many are the persons who have occasion to remember his kind professional services, given without hope of fee or reward.

John G. Stuart came July 1. He was born in Halifax,

N. S., February 10, 1834. He established the first wagon shop in Fort Scott.

T. W. Tallman and family arrived on the 22d of April, 1857. Mr. Tallman was taken at once for his true worth as a man. He has held many positions of trust and honor, with trust and honor. He went out in the world at sixteen to shift for himself, and after these long and busy years he feels that life has not been a failure.

Dr. A. G. Osbun came this year (1857). Governor Wilson Shannon married for his second wife Miss Sarah Osbun, sister of Dr. Osbun. Dr. Osbun took no active part in political affairs, but attended quietly to the duties of his profession. In the latter years of his life he was in partnership with Dr. Couch in the drug business.

Mrs. Osbun and the family of girls and boys came to the county the following year, after the doctor had located here.

The following named persons also came in to Fort Scott in 1857, most of whom came early in the year:

W. I. Linn, J. C. Sims, Dr. Bills and family, C. P. Bullock, S. B. Gordon, Joe Price, Governor E. Ransom, Receiver of the Land Office, his wife, son-in-law Geo. J. Clark and family; the notorious George W. Clark, Register of the Land Office, Tom Blackburn, Charley Bull, Charley Dimon, Orlando Darling, Joe Ray, W. B. Bentley, J. S. Calkins, J. E. Jones, A. R. Allison, J. N. Roach and family of girls, John Harris and family, H. R. Kelsoe and family.

The town at that time consisted entirely of the houses

around the Plaza, which had been built by the Government. No new buildings had yet been erected. Imagine the city, buildings, trees, etc., all cleared away and the wild, unbroken prairie in their stead coming clear up to the Plaza on all sides, and there you have Fort Scott as it appeared at that day.

The business houses were not yet very numerous. Colonel H. T. Wilson had the old post-sutler store, southwest of the Plaza, Blake Little & Son occupied the old quartermaster building, northwest corner of the Plaza, and Hill & Son were in the old guard house. There was one blacksmith shop and two saloons.

FORT SCOTT TOWN COMPANY.

About the 1st of June, 1857, a party arrived at Fort Scott, which had been made up at Lawrence, Kansas, consisting of Norman Eddy of Indiana, Geo. A. Crawford of Lock Haven, Pennsylvania, D. H. Weir of Indiana, and E. W. Holbrook of Michigan. Their purpose in coming to Fort Scott was, principally, to organize a town company. The town had been incorporated by act of the Legislature of 1855, as has been stated. A "Town Company" had already done some wind work and formed a "curbstone" organization, consisting of C. B. Wingfield, G. W. Jones, S. A. Williams and others. The Wingfield Company, as it was called, had no title to any land described in the act of the Legislature incorporating the "Town of Fort Scott," nor did anybody else. Claims had been filed on the different parts of sections by different parties, and the Wingfield company designed to acquire title to the townsite under the pre-emption laws.

On the 8th day of June, 1857, according to the original record, the Fort Scott Town Company "made conditional purchase, and took possession of the 'claims' known as the site of Fort Scott," and organized the company with the following named members: D. H. Weir, D. W. Holbrook, E. S. Lowman, W. R. Judson, G. W. Jones, H. T. Wilson, Norman Eddy, George A. Crawford and T. R. Blackburn.

The Wingfield organization was kept alive, however, with the view of holding good the pre-emption rights of the individual members, until, on the 5th day of January, 1858, at a meeting of the Fort Scott Town Company the following action was taken:

"Ordered, That the idea of attempting to pre-empt the property of the company under the two organizations of the Wingfield Company and the Fort Scott Town Company be formally abandoned. And that the members and interests of the Wingfield Company be in form, as they are in fact, received into and merged in the Fort Scott Town Company."

An outline of the early life of Mr. Crawford is given at this point. From the day of his arrival in Fort Scott his life is interwoven with the history of the town and Bourbon County.

George A. Crawford was born in Pine Creek Township Clinton County, Pennsylvania, on July 27, 1827. His ancestors were well known and active in the Revolution. He spent his boyhood in Clinton County, and received his higher education at Clinton Academy. After he had finished his education he went to Salem, Kentucky, where he taught school, and in 1847 he taught in the high schools of Canton, Mississippi. In 1848 he returned to Pennsylvania and studied law.

Mr. Crawford was active and quite prominent in the State politics of Pennsylvania, taking James Buchanan as his political guide, and later, his personal friend Stephen A. Douglas. And finally, in the latter days of the life of Douglas, joining with him in the hearty support of the Administration of President Lincoln.

As we have seen, in the spring of 1857, he came to Fort Scott, where he at once identified himself with the large Free-State immigration just then beginning to come in from the North. He was soon recognized and accepted as the head of the combined political sentiment of men from all sections of the country—North and South—who may be denominated, in the political shading of that time, as the conservative "Anti Pro-slavery party. He had, however, no better personal friends than he found among such men as Col. Wilson, A. Hornbeck, S. A. Williams, Blake Little, John H. Little, Col. Arnett, W. I. Linn and others then here, whose political prejudices were at that time in harmony with the great leaders of the South.

Mr. Crawford had a more extended acquaintance and close personal friendship with prominent men of the Nation than any man in the West. He was familiar with all sections and all men. Polished and peculiarly social in his manner, he was as much at home in the political and diplomatic circles of Washington as he was in the squatter's cabin. Had his inclinations been for a political career he could have easily attained great prominence. But the bent of his disposition was to be at the head of large commercial and manufacturing enterprises. For this, he chose this State and particularly Fort Scott as the basis of his operations. He succeeded well for several years, considering the disjointed period of civil war, and had laid the foundation of his future hopes. But circumstances, which so often attack the affairs of men, combined with the elements for his overthrow. He saw his mills and factories swept away by fire in an hour's time, leaving him struggling and helpless in the quick-sand of unrelentive fate. The divinity which shapes the affairs of men could come to him no more. It had passed by his door forever.

The lives of all men "are of few days and full of trouble." They pass like the shadow of a summer cloud. One falls; the ranks close up and move on, and only memory glances back. So with him.

His last resting place is in the Grand Canyons of the Colorado. His monument is the memory of those not yet fallen.

UNITED STATES OFFICERS.

The United States Land Office for this District was located at Fort Scott in the Spring of 1857. Epaphroditus Ransom was appointed Receiver, and G. W. Clark, under the name of Doak, was appointed Register.

On the 10th of July, Hon. Joseph Williams took the oath of office before Secretary Stanton, as Associate

Justice of the Territorial Supreme Court. He arrived at Fort Scott soon after, bringing with him his wife and four sons, Mason, Kennedy, Joseph and William, and immediately entered upon the duties of his office. He had lived many years in Muscatine and Burlington, Iowa, where he had been on the bench "twenty-one years a judge in Iowa" as he invariably instructed the jury in his charge. He was a weak man, easily influenced, and without personal dignity.

MORE TENDERFEET.

About the first of August, 1857, several more people arrived who were afterwards active and prominent citizens.

B. P. McDonald came to Fort Scott from Lock Haven, Pennsylvania. He was then a boy of 17. He took up a timber claim soon after his arrival here, and after the sawmill started he employed men in cutting and hauling logs to the mill where he worked as a hand himself, and from the proceeds of his lumber he made enough to start him in business with his brother, Alexander McDonald. In 1861 the firm of A. McDonald & Brother turned their attention to freighting in addition to their other mercantile business and afterwards added a banking department. In 1867 he purchased the entire business and continued it in his own name until 1869. He then closed out the business except the banking department, which he, with C. F. Drake and others afterward organized into the First National Bank. He was always foremost in aiding all railroad enterprises looking towards Fort Scott, and in 1874 he took hold individually of a railway project for a road in a southeastern direction from Fort Scott, and after completing a section of several miles he finally transfered it to the Kansas City, Fort Scott and Gulf Railroad Company, and his conception and original labors resulted in the construction of the great trunk line to Memphis, Tennessee.

Charles Bull had arrived sometime before. He was a youngish looking man then, and has maintained the same personal appearance for the past thirty years. He is now with the Zuna Indians. He was the most even tempered man in the Territory, always excepting Joe Ray.

Joseph Ray came from Michigan. He was another of the young men who came here to seek his fortune, only he didn't want any fortune except to be able to give to anybody and everybody in need. That was Joe. He was the life of any party or company, and had a smile and a joke for every one on every occasion. There is no man in the long list of the early settlers who have passed away whose memory is kept greener than is his.

William Gallaher arrived on the 1st of August from Illinois, originally from Pennsylvania. He was also quite a young man. He was, however, more lucky than some of the other boys, for he got a splendid situation soon after his arrival. He was appointed postmaster—the third one for Fort Scott—which position paid him over twenty-four hundred—cents a year. But he went into the army and lost it all.

Charles Dimon came from New York. Charley was a good fellow, but he had one bad habit, that was corns on his feet.

Ed. A. Smith, Burns Gordon, Albert H. Campbell and A. R. Allison were also boys of the class of '57. They all graduated with honor in that school the like of which will never again be opened. School is out, and the teacher is dead.

THE FREE STATE HOTEL.

The boys who came in this year and the men who had no families with them generally boarded at the Fort Scott Hotel, or the "Free State Hotel," as it was better known. It was under the management of Charley Dimon, with Ben McDonald and Charley Bull, and most any of the other boys, as clerks. Will Gallaher kept his postoffice there. This hotel was the building on the West corner of the Plaza, built by the Government for officers quarters, and now owned and occupied by Hon. William Margrave. It was first opened as a hotel by Col. Arnett soon after the post was abandoned in 1854, and was then the first and only hotel in the county. In the Spring of 1857, it was run by the Casey Bros. Later Charley Dimon took charge of it, and continued in it until January, 1859.

This house is a historical landmark. In 1857 it acquired the name of "The Free State Hotel," which it retained for many years. If its walls could talk it could beat this history all to pieces.

CHAPTER XI.

LECOMPTON CONSTITUTIONAL CONVENTION.

IT was now the beginning of autumn. The spring season had opened favorably for the farmers, and wherever they had been permitted to stay at home and work, the prospect was good for abundant crops. Everything seemed to be reasonably quiet in this part of the Territory, although it was a forced quiet, and there was much feeling of unrest and apprehension among the people.

The political talk was about the approaching Pro-slavery convention to frame a State Constitution, which was to be held at Lecompton.

As has been noted, the Legislature had passed an act providing for the election of delegates to this convention, on the 15th of June, 1857. The Free State men had, with something like concert of action all over the Territory, let the election of these delegates go by default. They felt that there was no chance for an expression of Free State opinions, and no guarantee that it would be anything but a repetition of the villainous frauds and outrages which had heretofore taken place under the name of "election."

The Free State men, however, began to realize that

immigration had in reality now placed their party in the majority. Their confidence and courage were strengthened, and hope renewed. But the delegates were already elected.

If the Free State men had taken prompt and vigorous measures to contest the election of June 15, attended to the registration and seen to it that the lists were corrected, and then mustered their forces at the polls with a determined front, it is possible that they might have elected a majority of the delegates, obtained control of the Lecompton Convention, presented a Free State Constitution to the people, who would have sustained it, and the State have quietly passed into the Union, and the pages of Kansas history been altogether changed.

The Convention met at Lecompton on the 7th of September, 1857. Blake Little and H. T. Wilson were the delegates chosen from this District. Little was chosen President pro tem. of the Convention.

After several adjournments the Convention finally completed their work on the 3rd of November, guarded by 200 U. S. troops. It was provided that the election on the adoption of this Constitution should be held on the 21st of December; that the question should be divided and that the ticket should read: "For the Constitution and Slavery," and "For the Constitution without Slavery."

The time for the regular meeting of the Territorial Legislature was January 4, 1858, but Acting Governor Stanton called an extra session which met on the 7th day of December, 1857, and passed an act providing for a vote on the entire constitution—a straight proposition for or against—to be held January 4, 1858, and providing more thoroughly against fraud.

The elections were quite numerous this fall and winter, and somewhat confusing unless attended to in their regular order.

THE ELECTION OF OCTOBER 5, 1857.

The election for members of the Territorial Legislature and for Delegate to Congress was held on the 5th of October.

E. Ransom, of Fort Scott, ran against Mark Parrott, the Free State candidate for delegate.

At this election there were again some indications of fraud, especially at the Oxford and Kickapoo precincts, and in McGee county. McGee county, for instance, "cast" 1202 Pro-slavery votes against 24 votes for the Free State ticket. Fraud was patent to every body. There were not a hundred legal voters in the county, all told. The original returns from McGee county were seen by one or more of our Fort Scott men before they were doctored and sent on to Lecompton. The lists contained a total of exactly eighty-three names.

At this election Bourbon County voted as follows: Drywood precinct, Ransom 9, Parrott 3; Russell precinct, Ransom 12, Parrott 2; Fort Scott precinct, Ransom 99, Parrott 24; Sprattsville precinct, Ransom 33, Parrott 47; Osage precinct, Ransom 22, Parrott 20. Total, Ransom 175, Parrott 96.

The Governor issued a proclamation on the 22d of October, rejecting the returns of the election precincts where the most glaring frauds had occurred. This reduced the total vote for Ransom to 3,799, as against 7,888 for Parrott, and the certificate of election was issued to Parrott, and he took his seat in Congress the next December.

George A. Crawford was the Democratic candidate for Territorial Council from this District, which consisted of Bourbon and seventeen other counties, McGee among them. Mr. Crawford went to Lecompton at once, and in a conference with Governor Walker and Secretary Stanton he advised the throwing out of the fraudulent votes, although such action defeated his own election.

MORE TROUBLE.

The wave of Free State immigration which had rolled in over the northern part of the Territory now began to reach down into Southern Kansas, and to be felt in Bourbon County to a greater extent than ever before. And the troubles which had prevailed in the North for so long a time were to be also transferred to the Southeastern border.

The Free State men who had been driven out in the summer and fall of 1856, now began to return—many of them coming back armed—and as they found that their strength had been materially increased by the considerable number of new settlers coming into the county they had confidence that by organization they could now maintain themselves and recover their claims and much of their other property. Among their leaders were J. C. Burnett, Samuel Stevenson, Captain Bain and Josiah Stewart.

Notice was served on those who had wrongfully taken possession of cabins and claims that they must leave. Many did so at once, but others relying on aid and assistance from the "Blue Lodges" of organized Pro-slavery men which existed in Fort Scott and along the border, refused to vacate.

As an illustration of those difficulties, the case of Stone and Southwood is given. William Stone had been driven off of his claim on the Osage, and his claim and cabin were taken possession of by a man named Southwood, a Southern preacher. When Stone returned to assert his rights Southwood refused to vacate. The Free State men, after considering the case, built Stone another cabin, near Southwood's, and moved his family into it. The women of the two families, of course, got into a small border war over the well of water. This helped to aggravate matters and the Free State men finally ordered Southwood to leave by a certain time. Just before the time fixed to leave, Southwood gathered a large number of his friends from Fort Scott and along the border with the purpose of driving Stone off. But the Free State men were right on hand, and gathered at Stone's to resist the expected attack. It was a first-rate opening for a good fight, but the Pro-slavery party, after a feint of an attack that night, drew off. They made much big talk, but they found the Free State party too strong and determined, and Southwood left.

The opposing forces, or factions, came near a collision several times after that. Things looked ugly. But for some reason the Pro-slavery men declined to open the ball, and the Free State policy was to await an attack.

Finally, a resort was had to the forms of "law." A term of the U. S. District Court was commenced on the 19th of October, 1857. It was held in the south room of the land office building, Judge Joseph Williams presiding, S. A. Williams, Clerk, and J. H. Little, Deputy U. S. Marshal. This court was in full sympathy and control of the Pro-slavery party. Claimants throughout the District took their cases before this court, and Judge Williams in most of the "claim cases" decided against the Free State man.

Free State men were often arrested on some trumped-up charge and were held for excessive bail or refused bail altogether. These arbitrary proceedings were very aggravating to them and they instituted a "court" of their own.

SQUATTER'S COURT.

What they called a "Squatter's Court" was organized for the District. A full complement of officers, Judge, Clerk, Sheriff, etc., was appointed. The first "court" was held at what was called "Bain's Fort," a large log house on the Osage river, a little northwest of the present town of Fulton. It was built by old John Brown and Captain Bain. Dr. Rufus Gilpatrick, of Anderson county, was Judge, and Henry Kilbourn, Sheriff. Here they tried causes in due form of law, and meted out justice according to their best light.

The only reasonable ground for "exceptions" to be taken to the proceedings was, perhaps, that as there was no family Bible handy the witnesses were sworn on "Dr. Gunn's Family Physician." But as this was a court from which there was no appeal, exceptions, though often taken, were rarely noted.

The existence of this rival court was not to be tolerated by Judge Williams and his friends, and on the 12th day of December, 1857, he ordered Deputy Marshal Little to organize a posse and dissolve it. Little went up there with a few men but the court failed to dissolve. On the 16th he again advanced on the works with a posse of about fifty men. When near the fort he was met by a party with a flag of truce headed by D. B. Jackman. They held a parley, and were finally informed by Little that if they did not surrender at once he would fire on them. The truce party warned Little that if he advanced it would be at his peril. They then returned to the fort, and Little advanced to the attack and opened fire. Several volleys were exchanged. The attack was repulsed. Some of Little's men and horses were slightly wounded. He then returned to Fort Scott. On the next day he increased his force to 100 men and returned again to the attack, but he found, on arriving at the fort, that the garrison had escaped during the night, and the court "adjourned."

One of the posse was named James Rhoades, who started back to Marmaton, where he had been employed in Ed. Jones' saw-mill. On the road he met a Mr. Weaver, a Free State man, and they got into a quarrel. Weaver was unarmed. Rhoades carried a loaded gun and was himself well loaded with that same old Missouri whiskey. In the quarrel he attempted to shoot Weaver, but Weaver got the gun away from him and killed him with it.

A little before this time a difficulty began between two of the Osage settlers. It was a claim fight. In 1856 a man named Hardwick came in there and took a claim. Isaac Denton and his sons, James and John Denton, came in about the same time. Hardwick permitted James Denton to occupy a cabin on his claim with the understanding that he was to vacate at a certain time. When the time came around Denton refused to vacate. Hardwick was threatened, his cabin was fired into, and he was forced to give up his claim and get out. Soon after this Isaac Denton and a friend and neighbor named Hedrick, were killed. Hardwick was suspected of the crime and he fled the country. A year or two afterwards he was arrested in Missouri for this crime and delivered to John Denton to be brought to Kansas for trial. On the way Denton shot Hardwick dead. Denton, in his turn, was killed at Barnesville, by Bill Marchbanks, for the killing of Hardwick.

A PROTECTIVE SOCIETY.

Geo. H. B. Hopkins settled on the Osage in September, 1856. He lived neighbor to Hedrick when the latter was called from the bed-side of his sick wife and shot down in his own door. The Dentons also lived in the same neighborhood. The killing of Hedrick and Denton on account of the threats of the Pro-slavery men that no Free State man should be allowed to raise a crop or stay on his claim, caused Mr. Hopkins and his neighbor, Mr. Denison, to start out and organize a "Protective Society." A large meeting was collected. Squire Jewell was made chairman. Hopkins, Jewell and Denison were chosen a committee to draft by-laws.

At a second meeting, three days later, James Montgomery of Linn County was present, but took no part until the men present at the meeting showed their hands by passing the following resolution:

"Resolved, That we, the members of this organization, pledge ourselves to protect all good citizens in their rights of life and property irrespective of politics."

Montgomery then arose and in a speech said: "I am now with you and will be to the end. Some men must be active in defense while others work. We have a hydra-headed monster to fight, and I for one will fight him and with his own weapons, if necessary." And from that time dated the activity of Montgomery as a partisan leader of the Free State men. He now proposed to take the saddle.

After Isaac Denton and Hedrick were killed, old man Travis, also a settler on the Osage, was arrested charged with having something to do with their murder. He was taken before the Squatter's Court at Mapleton and there found not guilty. On his way home he stopped at Dr. Wasson's, and that night the house was attacked and he was killed. Dr. Wasson was also shot in the arm and crippled for life. This was done or instigated by Jim Denton.

CHAPTER XII.

THE CONSERVATIVES.

ALL through these border troubles there was naturally and necessarily what may be called a conservative resident element in Fort Scott and throughout the county, of both the Pro-slavery and Free State parties; men trying to attend to business, improve their claims, make homes, and carry on their daily avocations. These men were, as they well expressed it, between two fires. And the alarms, incursions, excursions and the retaliatory acts, back and forth between the two parties were carried on over the heads of these law-abiding men. It was a difficult position, much harder to maintain in the country than in town. These men were not conservative in the sense of being non-committal or even non-partisan but as being "non-active" in the political difficulties which did not concern their private affairs.

It is of no avail to speculate now whether or not this factious, partisan border trouble was necessary or could have been prevented. It was simply a matter of fact; it existed, and that is all there is to be said about it. The Free State men were, in a large measure, on the defensive. They either had to hold their ground or be driven out. Get out or fight. It was a "condition and not a theory that confronted them," although it was a theory which, in some sense, had brought them to this country in the first place; the theory that they had a right to go into United States territory, take a claim, make a home and speak and vote as they pleased. And they proceeded at once on the theory that the condition they found was a theory, and that their original theory should become the condition.

U. S. TROOPS AT FORT SCOTT.

The constant alarms occurring in the latter part of this year resulted in the calling of a public meeting at Fort Scott on the 13th day of December. E. Ransom was made chairman. Resolutions were reported that a vigilance committee of five should be appointed to take measures to assist in the better execution of the law, either by the organization of a militia company or an appeal to the Governor and having United States troops stationed here. The committee appointed was H. T. Wilson, Blake Little, T. B. Arnett, G. A. Crawford and J. W. Head. The committee rightly concluded that it would be injudicious to try to organize a military company at that time, and decided to ask for troops, who were supposed to have no politics. At their instance John S. Cummings, the sheriff of the county, reported to Acting Governor Stanton that he required the aid of U. S. troops in the execution of the law, and sent the concurrent statement of Marshal Little to the same effect. In response to this request

Captain Sturgis, afterwards a Union General, was sent here on the 21st of December with Companies E. and F. 1st U. S. Cavalry, and order was restored and maintained for the short time they were here.

FIRST VOTE ON THE LECOMPTON CONSTITUTION.

Governor Walker, finding that his idea of fairness and justice ran counter to that of the propaganda, resigned his office on the 17th of December.

He had been absent from the Territory for some time and Secretary Stanton had been Acting Governor, and while so acting had called the special session of the Territorial Legislature to change the date and manner of voting on the Lecompton Constitution, and for that act, and others not in the programme, he was removed.

J. W. Denver was appointed to succeed him as Secretary, and took the oath of office on the 21st of December, and became Acting Governor.

On December 21, the first election was held on the Lecompton Constitution. At this election the Free State men again abstained from voting, or giving it any attention.

The vote in Bourbon County, as returned, was as follows:

For the Constitution, with slavery, ... 366
For the Constitution, without slavery, . . . 78

There were only nine votes cast against the constitution in the entire Territory. These were voted at Leavenworth and the tickets read "To hell with the Lecompton Constitution."

This election, besides being otherwise a farce, was more or less fraudulent in every precinct in the Territory, Bourbon County not excepted.

Bourbon County elected members of the State Legislature under the Lecompton Constitution as follows: Blake Little for Senator, D. W. Campbell and J. C. Sims for the House.

Efforts were now being made at different points, notably at Leavenworth, to organize a Free State Democratic party, as Free State Democrats everywhere repudiated the Lecompton Constitution, but no organization was effected in 1857.

Among the arrivals about the close of the year were Alex McDonald, brother of B. P. McDonald, and E. S. Bowen, who had purchased and shipped a sawmill, which was on the road and would arrive in due time. The mill machinery began to arrive about the middle of the next month, and was to be erected at a site chosen for it near the corner of what is now First Street and Ransom Street, or maybe a little further West towards Scott Avenue.

Lumber was going to be in demand, for building would begin in the Spring, although the year 1857 was closing in turmoil, excitement and uncertainty.

CHAPTER XIII.

SECOND ELECTION ON LECOMPTON CONSTITUTION.

THE year 1858 opened politically with the now almost periodical election on the Lecompton Constitution. This one occurred on the 4th of January, as was provided for, as will be remembered, by the Territorial Legislature in the special session of December, 1857.

In Bourbon County the vote was as follows:

For the Constitution with slavery 55
For the Constitution without slavery . . . none
Against the Constitution. 268

The total vote in the Territory, as published, was:

For the Constitution with slavery. 138
For the Constitution without slavery . . .   23
Against the Constitution 10,226

There was little or no deliberate or prearranged fraud in this election in Bourbon County. The Pro-slavery men in their turn abstained to a great extent from voting, but the Free State men went at it in great shape this time.

No analysis of the vote can be made. It will be noted that Bourbon County cast nearly one-half of the total votes in the Territory for the Constitution with slavery, as they were finally counted. But the vote proved nothing as to the relative strength of parties in this county. If an accurate poll of the legal voters in the county that day could have been taken for the Constitution with slavery, or against the entire Constitution, it would have resulted in about 250 votes for each side of the question.

FIRST NEWSPAPER ESTABLISHED.

The Fort Scott Town Company fell heir to the press and material of the "Southern Kansan," which was started and two numbers issued by Kline, who went to war, and got killed in 1856, as you have read.

This material was afterwards stored in the blacksmith shop of Arnett's corral, where it remained until January, 1858, when it was resurrected under the auspices of J. E. Jones. It was removed to the south room of the second floor of the Land Office building, where Joe Williams, jr., and Charlie Bull—scrub typos, proceed to sort the pi, and make ready for the publication of the Fort Scott *Democrat*. The first number of the *Democrat* made its appearance on the 27th of January, 1858, J. E. Jones, editor.

The publication of the *Democrat* was continued by Mr. Jones until sometime in 1859, when he left town.

THE FIRST GRAND BALL.

About the 1st of January, 1858, W. T. Campbell, who with his family, had been living at Barnesville, whither he had moved from Kalamazoo, Michigan, came to town and took charge of the Fort Scott or Free State Hotel. Soon after, he gave what might be termed the opening ball. All the elite of the city were present. One fiddle furnished the music. Joe Ray "called," and "alamand left" was heard at regular intervals until the "wee sma' hour" of seven o'clock next morning. We don't remember very well all the ladies who were there, but we do remember Miss Jemima Roach. Jemima was the belle of the evening. For the benefit of the rising generation we will give something of a description of her ball costume, which will answer for a description of all, for they were all about alike—cut off the same piece in Colonel Wilson's store. Well, Jemima had on a good warm linsey woolsey dress, with small check, say, half-inch square, cut high neck and low sleeves, trimmed with a feathery ruche of cut calico, and a dove colored belt, a la cinch Mexicano. We believe the dress was not cut bias anywhere, unless it was under the arms. Just a good plain every day dress that would do to milk in. Then good warm woolen stockings, Government red tape garters, and good stout calf-skin shoes, laced with buckskin strings. That's all. Sally Duncan was the only one known to complain about a thing at the ball. She said she "didn't like the durned abolition callin'; too much cheatin' yer pardners."

TROUBLE BEGINS AGAIN.

The troops remained here until the 10th of January. 1858, when they were ordered away, and then trouble commenced again. Some of the Border Ruffians took a squad out to where Mr. Johnson lived and abused him, took some of his stock, and threatened to make him leave. Johnson got word to Montgomery about it, and asked him to come down and see about some fellows whose names he gave as the leaders, who were then stopping in Fort Scott. About the 10th of February Montgomery was sighted by some of their scouts, coming in sure enough, with a party of twenty men. Out about the California ford on the Marmaton they were met by a delegation to ascertain what he wanted. When he told them who he was after, they informed him that this particular man had leaked out into Missouri. But Monty thought he would come in and see for himself. So he did. But they were gone. Then Crawford and Judge Williams and some others, invited him and his forces to take breakfast at the Free State Hotel; presented him the freedom of the city, so to speak—on a tin platter. So the boys, who were in their "working clothes," and not overly well dressed, took on a good breakfast, and then went quietly home.

On the 15th, the men Montgomery had been looking for returned, Brockett among them. Soon after that a difficulty occurred between Brockett and Charley Dimon, which might have resulted seriously, had it not been for the firmness and courage of Colonel Campbell.

OBJECT LESSON IN SURGERY.

On the 28th of February a party under command of Dr. Jennison and "Rev." Stewart, alias "Plum," went to the house of a Pro-slavery man named Van Zumwalt, on the Osage, and routed him out. When the door was being opened—which was hung on wooden hinges and opened outward—the muzzle of a gun was noticed being poked out through the crack near the upper hinge. Some one shot at it and Van received the ball in his arm. He then surrendered. It was found to be a bad wound, and Jennison, who was a very good surgeon, then went to work and washed and dressed the wound, giving the boys a clinical lecture as he went along, explaining everything, and giving them instructions how to proceed in similar cases which were likely to to occur in the future.

If Van had been killed it is presumed Rev. Stewart would have made a "few remarks" about the uncertainty of this life, and said a few words for the repose of his soul.

The Jayhawkers always went well fixed in the matter of the learned professions. They generally had a doctor and a preacher along, and quite often a lawyer.

ORIGIN OF "JAYHAWKER."

On this trip the word, Jayhawker, originated. Jennison had with him a regular all-around thief named Pat Devlin. After the boys went into camp north of the Osage, the next morning after visiting Van Zumwalt, they noticed Pat coming in riding a yellow mule loaded down with all sorts of plunder. In front of him were hanging from the horn of the saddle, a big turkey, three or four chickens and a string of red peppers, behind him a 50-pound shoat, a sheep-skin, a pair of boots and a bag of potatoes.

"Hello, Pat, where have you been," asked Doc.

"O'ive been over till Eph. Kepley's a-jayhawking."

"Jayhawking? What in thunder do you mean? What kind of hawking is that?" said Doc.

"Well, sor, in ould Oireland we have a birud we call the jayhawk, that whin it catches another birud it takes deloight in bullyragin the loife out ov it, like a cat does a mouse, and, be jasus, Oi bethot me Oi was in about thot same business mesilf. You call it 'foraging off the inemy,' but, begobs, O'ill call it jayhawking."

"All right," laughed Jennison. "We'll call it 'Jayhawking' from this on." And so it was.

This same Pat Devlin took a claim on the Osage some time before the incident related, laid a foundation for a cabin on it and prepared for pre-emption. But his inclination to jayhawk overcame any desire he may have had to become a farmer, and, in consequence, he was away so much "on thot business" that he forfeited all right to his claim. John Hinton, of the Osage, then jumped the claim, built a cabin and moved his father and mother and family into it. Among the family was the old grand father, a man about 85 years of age, who was bed-ridden and helpless from rheumatism. One day Pat was riding by the cabin, and on examination, he found that the family were all away from home except the old man. What did he do then but turn in and first tearing the roof off the house he rolled the logs off one at a time clear down to a level with the old grand pap's bed, leaving him there in the weather, alone and utterly helpless.

CHAPTER XIV.

FIRST MANUFACTORY IN FORT SCOTT.

ABOUT the 20th of February, 1858, McDonald's saw-mill was completed and steamed up for the first time. The boys thought this was a proper occasion to steam up likewise, and Alex. McDonald "gave a party" that night. Egg-nog was the principal ingredient. Ben. McDonald, John Little and Ed. Smith were chief cooks and did the mixing. They thought they had plenty of fuel when they started in, but Ben said they run out of Polk County sour mash, and towards the last he had to chuck in some bay rum. Anyway, they laid the boys all out, bottom side up. They didn't know whether they were border ruffians or prohibitionists. Joe Ray said the next day, they had to dust their hats with slick powder and put them on with a shoe horn.

The boys had lots of fun at this saw-mill. Ben was head sawyer and Joe "bore off" the slabs, when he couldn't get Charlie Osbun, or some one of the other boys to do it for him. Joe wasn't lazy, but he was awful tired. They sawed cottonwood lumber sometimes. Cottonwood was great lumber to warp. Joe said it would often curl up and crawl off in the bushes and hide.

MARMATON TOWN COMPANY.

On the 6th of February, 1858, an act was passed by the Legislature incorporating the town of Marmaton. W. R. Griffith, W. B. Barber, W. H. Krotzer and Horatio Knowles were named as the incorporators. On the 11th of February another act was passed incorporating the Town Company of Marmaton. The incorporators were T. R. Roberts, J. E. Jones, Orlando Darling and Charles Dimon. This Company spelled the name with an "i" instead of an "a" thus: "Marmiton." The correct way to spell the name of the town and the river is as the Town Company had it. The name was given the river by the French fur traders who were here before any other white people. The word means scullion, or kitchen boy, the one that empties the pots and slops. But the people of the town and township preferred to spell the name "Marmaton," and they petitioned the County Court to have the spelling of the name changed, and it was so ordered.

UNIONTOWN.

Uniontown was laid out in 1858, by Aleph Goff, W. W. Wright and B. F. Gumm, who were members of the Town Company. Uniontown took the place of "Turkey Creek" post office, which was a well known point in the early days of the Territory, when it was in "Russell" Township. It is surrounded by as fine an agricultural country as there is in the county, and the settlers, old and new, are of the best class of people.

THE LEAVENWORTH CONSTITUTION.

The Legislature on the 10th of February, 1858, passed an act providing for the election of delegates to another State Constitutional Convention. The election was held on the 9th of March. W. R. Griffith was delegate from this county. The Convention met at Minneola on the 23rd of March, and after organizing adjourned to Leavenworth, where the first session was held on the 25th of March. On April 3d the "Leavenworth Constitution" was completed. The prominent feature of this Constitution was that it nowhere contained the word "white."

The Leavenworth Constitution did not figure to a great extent in the history of Kansas. President Buchanan had, on the 2nd of February, 1858, transmitted the old Lecompton Constitution to the Senate and recommended the admission of the State under it. This he did in the face of the known and often expressed opposition to that Constitution by both the Free State Republicans and the Free State Democrats.

THE ENGLISH BILL.

Congress, being unable to agree on the question, finally appointed a conference committee, and on the 23d of April, W. H. English, of Indiana, reported for the committee what is known as the "English Bill." This act provided that the Lecompton Constitution be again resubmitted to a vote of the people; provided stringent regulations for securing a fair vote, and provided for an immense grant of lands to the State for various purposes, aggregating nearly six million acres, as a straight bribe to the people if they would adopt it. We will vote on this proposition as quick as we can get around to it.

JAYHAWKING REDUCED TO PLAIN STEALING.

Everything being somewhat quiet this winter in the "political" circles of this section, Montgomery decided to retire from the field, and do a little work in the way of improvements on his farm in Linn county when spring opened. There were others, he thought, who could continue the watch on the border and keep the upperhand of the Border Ruffians in this part of the Territory. The man principally relied on to do that was a Methodist preacher called Captain, or "Rev." Stewart, the same man mentioned as having had a hand in the Van Zumwalt affair. Stewart had about twenty men, who mostly lived north of the Osage river, when they had any home at all. For awhile everything went off all right. But very soon brother Stewart "backslid," and he and his gang began stealing horses right and left, and running them off up north. They gave themselves up to plundering, robbing and stealing from everybody and anybody. They pretended to be Free-State men—called themselves so—but any man who had a little property was a Pro-slavery man in their eyes, and "all horses were Pro-slavery."

They committed so many villainous outrages that the settlers, of all parties, began to leave the country. Many came in to Fort Scott for protection. It seemed like the country would be depopulated. The Governor was appealed to for troops by Judge Williams and others, and on the 26th of February Captain George T. Anderson came down with two companies of the 1st U. S. Cavalry. But he could not do much good; he could not guard each individual, and he could not catch the thieves. He told the settlers who applied to him for protection that they must come in to Fort Scott. That was a difficult matter, too, for those who had property, especially stock. They could not well bring that in to town. This plundering and stealing was aided and participated in to some extent by a few of these very U. S. soldiers, who were sent here to protect the people. Edward Wiggin, who now lives on his farm about four miles north of Fort Scott, came here with Capt. Geo. T. Anderson, as a private in Company "I," Anderson's company. He says there was a small squad of his company, giving their names as Bill DeBost, Jim Simmons, Henry Sadwick and some others, who soon fell in with the idea of playing "Jayhawker," and influenced by some of the old Border Ruffians, repeatedly made stealing raids out into the county, in which they represented themselves as "Stewart's men," and Free-State men. A. Hyde, who after the war located in Fort Scott, and was at one time City Marshal, and who our citizens familiarly called Cap. Hyde, was also a member of Anderson's company. Through the influence principally of Ed. Wiggin and Cap. Hyde the thieves mentioned were driven out of the company for this stealing business.

In the meantime, all this thieving and indiscriminate

plundering was casting an odium on the Free State party and giving it a bad name among those who were not in the saddle.

Things came to such a pass that Montgomery again took the field to straighten them out. As soon as he appeared Stewart and most of his gang left this part of the Territory for a while and that sort of business ceased for some time.

FIGHT WITH U. S. TROOPS.

Montgomery remained in the field. The Southeastern border was infested by Border Ruffians of the worst class, many of whom had been driven down by the Free State men further north and had lodged along the Missouri State line. They were making their last stand here. Hamilton was their General-in-chief. It was an idea of theirs to use the United States troops to accomplish the capture of old Jim Montgomery. They had out their spies, and on the 21st of April it was ascertained and reported to them that Montgomery was in the Marmaton valley. Captain Anderson was at once urged by the Border Ruffian crowd to go out and bring him in. Anderson, like many of the regular army officers, was himself an ultra Pro-slavery man and would have liked nothing better than to have gotten hold of Montgomery. He did not require much urging, and soon started out with a detail of men to capture him. About six or eight miles out, in the Isaac Mills neighborhood, they sighted old Jim sure enough, riding leisurly along, with about twenty men,

WESTERN HOUSE, OR PRO-SLAVERY HOTEL.

NARROW DEFILE ON PAINT CREEK. 1858.

and they took after him full tilt. It had not yet become customary to fight United States troops by either faction, and Montgomery having no desire to commence the practice "skeedaddled." But being close pressed he turned up Yellow Paint Creek to a good narrow defile for defensive purposes which he knew of, quickly dismounted his forces to fight as infantry, and coolly awaited the onslaught of Anderson's troops. Anderson paid no attention to the order, three times given, to halt, but opened fire without dismounting, badly wounding one man, John Denton. Montgomery replied with a volley, killing one soldier named Alvin Satterwait, wounding one or two others and killing a soldier's horse, which fell on him pinning him to the ground, and also killing Anderson's horse. The regulars then retreated to town, and the irregulars went on about their business.

This was the first and only time United States troops were fired on during the border troubles. The Free State party had always been careful to avoid placing themselves in the light of rebels, or as resisting the bogus Territorial laws. This affair was not similar to that of Thermopolyae or the Alamo, for "'Thermopolyae had one messenger of destruction; the Alamo had none," but it might easily have been, had Anderson's force been of similar disproportion.

Captain Anderson resigned soon after this, and when the war broke out he went into the rebel army and became a Brigadier General. He had a brigade at Pittsburg Landing. Captain Hyde was also in that battle as a private in the regular army. On the first day of the battle Hyde was wounded and left in the hands of the Confederates, where he was accidentally thrown into the presence of General Anderson. They knew each other at once, and Anderson caused him to be taken care of until the second day, when the tide of battle, surging past where he was, left him in the hands of his friends.

The second in command under Montgomery in the Paint Creek fight was Aaron D. Stevens, then going under the name of Captain Whipple. More will be said of him hereinafter.

CHAPTER XV.

SOME OLD SETTLERS.

AMONG the men who settled in this county in the Spring of 1858, was James F. Holt, who went out to where William Holt was located on Turkey Creek. Mr. Holt was born in Tennessee, April 15, 1819. He was postmaster at Turkey Creek, and held other important positions and was a well known figure in our county affairs. William Jackman came from Pennsylvania and settled at Rockford. Guy Hinton, A. Wilson and his brother M. Wilson came out from Ohio, and located at Mapleton. Frank M. Smith, from Tennessee, settled near Mapleton. Charles Elliott, from Ohio, was quite a prominent man; he served as County Treasurer one term. D. B. Jackman, Attorney-at-Law, first went to Anderson county, but located "all along the Osage" in 1858. He was prominent in "Squatter Court" affairs. E. G. Jewell and D. Jewell settled on the Osage. E. G. Jewell, a very prominent man, was one of the vice-presidents at the organization of the Republican party at Osawatomie, May 18, 1859. H. Hickson, from Ohio, settled on Mill Creek. W. R. Clyburn, from Indiana, settled on Drywood. The Custard family, from Pennsylvania, and

J. B. Caldwell from the same State, settled on Drywood.

C. H. Haynes and family as noted by the Fort Scott *Democrat*, arrived in March, 1858. He soon afterwards purchased an interest in the saw-mill, and some time afterwards he and Mr. Jenkins moved the mill to the Marmaton river, northeast of the Plaza. Captain Haynes entered the service at the beginning of the war, as a lieutenant in the 6th Kansas, and in 1862 raised and commanded Co. B, 14th Kansas. He was married to Miss Jennie Hoyle, December 20, 1855.

John J. Stewart, who has already been mentioned as having come here in January, 1856, had now grown to manhood, and taken a claim on Mill Creek near Centerville. He married Miss Elizabeth Harbin in February, 1856. During the war he served first in the 6th Kansas, and afterwards raised and commanded Co. C, of Colonel Eaves' battalion, and was all through the Price raid of October, 1864. He has repeatedly represented the Mill Creek District in the Legislature, and has served two terms as County Treasurer. He finally moved to Fort Scott, and was one of the principal founders of the well known State Bank.

Charles W. Goodlander arrived in Fort Scott on the 29th of April, 1858. He came in on the first trip of the stage on the line between Kansas City and Fort Scott, just opened by Squires of Squireville, and which was to try to run tri-weekly thereafter. Goodlander had learned the carpenter trade, and desired to work at that business here; but not finding work just then, he took the job of carrying the mail to Cofachique, which then existed near where Humboldt is now. On his trip he found the postmaster at Turkey Creek away from home, and the lady of the house, Mrs. Holt, was washing. She gave him the key and told him to change the mail himself. He did so, and found the mail consisted of one lone copy of the N. Y. *Tribune*. He got an occasional job at his trade, and would often carry the necessary lumber from the sawmill on his back. After a while he built a shop of his own. He felt then like he was an independent citizen, and dreamed of the time in the far distant future when he would be worth a fortune of ten thousand dollars. That was the objective point which he hoped some day to attain. Like a good number of the men who came to Bourbon County in an early day who are recognized as among the leading citizens in the town and county, he was a poor boy, with only industry, integrity, native will power and good hard sense as the capital with which he commenced life. And like these men also, with whom he has often joined hands in local enterprises after the hardships of those disjointed times, he soon became a powerful factor in the advancement of the interests of the city and county.

E. L. Marble and Robert Blackett were already here. George Dimon, Dick Phillips and A. F. Bicking arrived in April, 1858.

IMPROVEMENTS BEGIN.

For a good while there was not much business going on in Fort Scott, and the young men found it difficult to get steady work. They did what they could find to do in the way of odd jobs, and when business got too slack and collections slow, they would "accept a position" on the jury of the United States Court. That was richness. The pay was $2.50 a day in gold.

All the boys resorted to the jury when it became necessary to make a payment on board and washing, especially board. The washing didn't worry them. The jury was about the only means of raising ready cash.

The saw mill had been running since the "opening night," sawing up oak logs into flooring and dimension stuff, and large walnut logs that would now be worth $100 each, into siding and fencing. The cottonwood lumber was all corralled or lariated out.

Building operations now commenced on Market street. W. I. Linn was the first to begin. He built and opened a saloon in the structure afterwards occupied by Linn & Stadden as a grocery store. J. S. Calkins put up a small building further east, and the town company another, opposite the head of Scott avenue, and alongside the alley running toward the corral. George J. Clarke and Will Gallaher also erected a small log building on the rear of the lot afterwards occupied by Riggins. Further out, Roach had erected the celebrated "Fort Roach." Ben. McDonald and Albert Campbell built a small house on Williams, street. Market street, then Bigler street, was not opened for some time, owing to Ben Hill's lot fence. His house was on the street, back of the Western Hotel. J. C. Linn commenced, but never completed, a three-story frame on the corner now occupied by the stone block on Wall and Main streets. Kelly's blacksmith shop stood on the point of the triangle between Wall and Market streets.

RUFFIANS HAVE AN INNING.

During the winter and early spring of 1858 there was much friction between Free-State men in Fort Scott and the ultra Pro-slavery party. The latter formed themselves into a secret society called the "Bloody Reds," which extended into the border counties of Missouri. Dr. George P. Hamilton was the head. The Western Hotel, then known better as the "Pro-slavery Hotel," was their "official" headquarters, although their favorite meeting place was at the house of Thomas Jackson, in Vernon County, Missouri. The Pro-slavery Hotel—now torn down—was on the opposite corner of the Plaza, directly facing the Free-State Hotel.

The "Reds" had a special spite against George A. Crawford, Will Gallaher and Charles Dimon, and they decided to commence operations by driving them out of town. On the 27th of April they received the following note addressed to them:

'GENTLEMEN:—You are respectfully invited to leave town in twenty-four hours.
"GEO. P. HAMILTON."

Crawford sent this verbal answer: "I don't exchange messages with horse-thieves," and the crisis was on. There was no longer room for both factions. One or the other must go. The Free State party, numbering about twenty-five well armed men, decided they would stay, fight all comers and take the chances. Both parties assembled at the Free State and Pro-slavery hotels, respectively, and neither ventured out. · B. F. Brantley and J. H. Little called on the Free State party and informed them that if the worst came they could count on them. But they felt doubtful about the soldiers, as, it will be remembered, Montgomery had killed one of them only a few days before, but E. A. Smith went into their camp and ascertained that they would at least remain neutral. Nevertheless, Brockett had secured three of them and secreted them in the Western Hotel. But the next day they were arrested and taken to camp under guard.

This state of affairs continued until the next night, when the "Reds" raised the siege, and the most of them left, never to return, and were not heard of again until the Marais des Cygnes massacre, in which they were the leading actors.

THE MARAIS DES CYGNES MURDER.

The Marais des Cygnes massacre occurred on the 19th of May, near the Trading Post. A body of twenty-five Border Ruffians, under the leadership of Captain Hamilton swooped down on the valley of Mine Creek, in Linn County, and gathering up eleven Free State men took them across the Marais des Cygnes river to a lonely ravine, formed them in line, and repeatedly fired into them, killing five outright and leaving all for dead.

Ten of these Border Ruffians were well-known in Fort Scott. They were the Hamiltons, W. B. Brockett.

Thomas Jackson, Harlan, Yealock, Beach, Griffith and, Matlock. The others were probably here more or less but their names are not certainly known.

The Marais des Cygnes murder was in some respects the most atrocious that had yet occurred in the Territory. It was a blow from organized extermination. The effect of this murder in the North was very great. It was taken up with more than usual feeling by the press, and the details were read in every Northern household. It was the blazing text of orators and the burning theme of poets. Altogether, it did much to shatter the elements of conservatism in the North, and shape a final crisis.

The nearest a parallel was the Pottawatomie murders committed by old John Brown and his sons, on the 24th of May, 1856. Brown went to the houses of his victims in the dead of night, and killed them one at a time. The men killed, five in number, were also unwarned and unarmed. It is true they were Pro-slavery men, but—a third of a century has passed away.

The actors of that time have taken their rightful places in public estimation. As for old John Brown, the prediction of his intimates did not take place that "the gallows would become as glorious as the Cross."

About the time of the massacre Montgomery was in Johnson County, but arrived that night at the Trading Post, where he found about 200 men assembled. The next morning a pursuit was organized with Sheriff McDaniels, R. B. Mitchell and Montgomery at the head. They left for West Point, a town about twelve miles north, where it was believed Hamilton had taken refuge. But they failed to find any of the gang, but it is believed some of them were there hidden away by the citizens. Search has kept up and the border guarded for sometime.

That fall Matlock was captured and taken to Paris, Linn County, for trial, but he escaped. In 1863 Wm. Griffith was arrested in Platte County, Missouri, and taken to Mound City for trial. He plead "not guilty" and set up the Amnesty Act as defense, but the jury found him guilty, and Judge S. O. Thatcher of this district sentenced him to death, and he was hanged October 30, 1863. Asa Hairgrove, one of the survivors of the massacre, acted as hangman.

THE EFFECT ON THE BORDER.

After the Marais des Cygnes murder the people all along the border were naturally much excited. They felt that this massacre was, in some sense, different and more alarming than any outrage that had yet occurred. They were used to hearing of murders, collisions between two factions, the sacking of towns, and of assassinations, but in these cases they were often the outcome of personal difficulties, or the animus was directed against persons or communities particularly objectionable. In this instance, however, they saw this armed band, sweeping in a semi-circle through the country, picking up one at a time these men who were absolutely inoffensive and driving them to slaughter. It looked to them like their enemy was organizing for a forlorn hope, a last final struggle, the delivery of the last venomous stroke of expiring energy. They did not know the day they, themselves, might not receive the stroke. Their fears were not altogether groundless. It is now known that this was only the first act of a pre-arranged plan for general murder and destruction.

The people felt much incensed against Fort Scott. The citizens of the town had, however unwillingly, permitted these Border Ruffians to make it their regular stopping place and silently acquiesced in the establishment of their headquarters. The stigma naturally attached itself.

The Governor, it is thought, realizing that there might be retaliatory measures taken by the Free State people, which must result in innocent bloodshed, had for that reason ordered a Deputy United States Marshal down to arrest Montgomery, or any other probable leader in such movement, and thus nip it in the bud. At any rate, Deputy Marshal Sam Walker was sent down here and arrived at Rayville on the 29th of May, with writs for Montgomery and some others. When he got to Rayville he found a large body of men who were being addressed by Montgomery in favor of proceeding to Fort Scott and executing vengeance on some few still there who were then believed to have been implicated with, and known to be in sympathy with the Hamilton crowd. On looking the ground over and feeling the sense of the people, Walker saw that was not the time or place to arrest Montgomery. But he made himself known, and, addressing the meeting, he informed them that if they would get out warrants for the arrest of G. W. Clark and others and furnish him with a posse, he would go to Fort Scott and make the arrests. The reply was that Judge Williams would not issue the writs. He told them to get warrants from a justice of the peace then, and, although it might not be strictly legal, he would arrest the parties nevertheless. This proposition was acted upon. He was furnished with the warrants and a posse of forty-four men. Montgomery went along. On Sunday morning, May 30th, they entered Fort Scott, found G. W. Clark, and after considerable bluster on his part, arrested him. By this time Clark's friends had assembled in considerable force, and Montgomery, knowing there were writs out for his arrest, concluded it would be discretion for him to "leak out." A demand was now made by Clark's friends that Mongomery be pursued and arrested. Walker, after consulting with Captain Nathaniel Lyon, who was then stationed here, and then present, decided to do so. He turned his prisoner over to the military, overtook Montgomery and brought him back. After Clark's friends had taken a good look at "Old Jim Montgomery," Walker left with him for Lecompton for trial. But at Rayville he was overtaken by a courier from Lyon informing him that Clark had been released by Judge Williams. This action disgusted and angered Walker, and he immediately turned Montgomery loose.

At the time Clark was arrested feeling was running very high. It was critical. Had Clark seriously resisted arrest, Walker would have killed him, when Walker would in turn have been riddled, and there is no telling where it would have stopped.

CHAPTER XVI.

AMNESTY.

GOVERNOR J. W. DENVER, on the 9th day of June, 1858, left Lecompton for a trip down the border, with a view of making a personal effort for the conciliation of the people. He was accompanied by Charles Robinson, Judge John C. Wright, A. D. Richardson and others. On their road down they visited James Montgomery at his home in Linn county, and he joined their party there.

They arrived at Fort Scott on the 13th. On the next day, the 14th, a public meeting was held on the Plaza, in front of the Free State Hotel. The people had generally been notified that the Governor would be here for the purpose of trying to arrive at a basis for a treaty, and if possible to conclude terms of peace between the factions, and to agree on an amnesty for all past political offenses against the law by men of both parties. It seemed like every man in the county was there. The Governor had asked to meet them, and they came, but they, as well as the people of the town, were distrustful and excited.

Governor Denver made the first speech in a quieting and conciliating tone and manner, which had a good effect. He was followed by Judge Wright, of Lawrence, and B. F. Brantley, of Fort Scott, in the same strain. After they got through Gov. E. Ransom took the stand. Ransom was quite an old man. He had been Governor of Michigan, and was a man of more than ordinary intelligence, although narrow-minded and bigoted in his views, and had always been thoroughly Pro-slavery in feeling. He began his speech by a terrific denunciation of the Free State people for having brought on the condition of affairs that then existed. He had only fairly started on this tirade when he was interrupted by Judge Wright who stepped in his front, facing him, and denied the statements he was making in a very sharp and emphatic manner. Governor Denver, whose attention had been called away for a moment, then sprang in between them, and sharply told them that sort of thing must stop, and speaking to Ransom, he said: "Governor Ransom, you are a much older man than I. I did not expect this kind of conduct on your part; I had a right to expect something different from you. You must stop that kind of talk. You must take your seat and be quiet." And he did take his seat, and kept quiet.

This account is in Governor Denver's own words. In an address published by the State Historical Society, Governor Denver continues the account of this day's proceedings as follows:

"To make a long story short, I prevailed upon all the county officers of Bourbon County to resign their offices, and then I told the people, that while I had the right to appoint any man I pleased to fill the vacancies, that I desired an expression of their wishes in the matter, and that I wanted them to hold an election right then and there, and that I would receive it as instructions as to whom to appoint to those offices. They asked me how they should do it. I told them to set up their candidates, place them out at one side of the public square, one here and another there, and let their friends form a line on the right and on the left. They placed their candidates out, and I gave the word to march. The people then formed. I then appointed two men to count them. They then counted them and reported to me the number they had found for each candidate. The first was for Sheriff, I think. Then for the next office we went through the same ceremony, and the election was held in that way. I gave them a certificate of appointment, and as soon as I got back to Lecompton I sent them their commissions."

This was a critical day in Fort Scott. The men of all parties and shades of politics, Border Ruffian, Jayhawker, Pro-slavery, ultra radical Abolitionists, Free State Republicans and Free State Democrats were all here together and facing each other. Before the speaking they had already began to divide and separate into parties, and at that moment the exchange of hot words or any offensive act would have precipitated a bloody battle.

The officers "elected" that day were as follows: For Sheriff, Thomas R. Roberts; for County Commissioners, or County Supervisors, as they were called, Thomas W. Tallman of Fort Scott, M. E. Hudson of Mapleton, Bryant Bauguess of Drywood, Jacob J. Hartley and Joab Teague of Marmaton. These men were given certificates of election by the Governor, who afterwards sent them their commissions from Lecompton.

At the first meeting of the Board, held soon after, Horatio Knowles was appointed Clerk of the Board, and some townships were organized.

PROTOCOL OF PEACE.

After the election the meeting was adjourned to meet at Rayville on the next day. At Rayville Governor Denver addressed the crowd, and after the speech he proposed the following as a basis for a treaty of peace:

1. Withdrawal of troops from Fort Scott.
2. The election of new officers for Bourbon County without reference to party.
3. Troops to be stationed along the State line to guard against invasion from Missouri.
4. Suspension of the execution of old writs until their legality be authenticated by the proper tribunal.
5. Montgomery and his men, and all other bodies of armed men on both sides to abandon the field and disperse.

After Governor Denver had concluded, Montgomery was called for. Montgomery was recognized as the party of the second part by the treaty making powers; the leading and representative spirit of the aggressive and self-protecting element of the Free State men of Bourbon County. The men at this meeting were not a band of marauders. They were men who lived and intended to continue to live in this county, and they had determined to have peace if they had to fight for it.

There was a hush of intense interest when Montgomery took the stand.

He immediately accepted the terms of the Governor's proposition. He continued, thanking the Governor for the interest he had taken in their affairs, the evident spirit of justice by which he seemed to be actuated; that peace, so long a stranger to this part of the country, was above all things, what he and the people most desired, and that if the Governor redeemed the pledges that day made, he would retire to his cabin and use his best efforts to prevent any further trouble.

The moderate Pro-slavery men, and the more conservative men of all parties were satisfied with the amnesty, as they called it, and for several months all seemed to strive to preserve the peace and tranquility which was thus restored.

MONTGOMERY SIZED UP.

James Montgomery in the general estimation of the people, is often rated and classed with J. H. Lane, John Brown and C. R. Jennison. He ought not to be so held. He was a different kind of a man. Their lives were in no ways parallel. He was no coward, assassin, crank, fanatic or murderer.

"He wore no knife to slaughter sleeping men."

His sincere desire was to see Kansas a free State. He was in spmpathy and co-operation with the men who made Kansas a free State. He was an instrument of the men who were holding at bay that party and that principle which were attempting to force slavery upon Kansas by the most outrageous violation of all personal and political rights. He was of the Free State party who were "holding the fort until the Republican party could arrive."

CHAPTER XVII.

SOME MORE ARRIVALS.

IN the first part of June, 1858, William Smith and wife arrived at Fort Scott with their son William H. and daughter Mary. The elder son, Edward A., was already here. Mr. Smith was born in Edinburgh, Scotland, in 1810. He was a printer by trade and worked for some years for Harper Bros. in New York, after his arrival in this country in 1830. "Uncle Billy Smith" was a man of strong, sturdy qualities, somewhat "set in his way," but with a large heart and warm sympathies. His wife, "Aunt Jane," was a noble, Christian woman. Mrs. Smith, with Mrs. Alec McDonald, organized the first Presbyterian church in Fort Scott, in the next November after their arrival.

John F. White came early in June, from Pennsylvania. He was absent from Fort Scott most of the time for two years or more, conducting the general store of George A. Crawford & Co., at the Trading Post. Then he returned and opened a store of his own. He was afterward, County Treasurer for four years. Jack was a noble man.

Charles F. Drake arrived June 17, 1858, from Mt.

Vernon, Ohio. He came just after the Denver meeting and compromise, having walked into town from the Osage, and arrived here dusty, ragged and hungry. Finding a rather peaceful condition of things just then he decided to remain, and soon after started a small hardware store and tin-shop, the first one in Southern Kansas. Thus he commenced pounding and soldering together the elements of his successful future. He, however, always found time to "be into" and help engineer nearly all the enterprises which have since been inaugurated in Fort Scott.

Our railroad enterprises have all felt the necessity of having the assistance of C. F. Drake, and most of them his signature also. He placed the Foundry on its feet and held it up for some years. He built the first Cement works, aided in the details by A. H. Bourne, Dr. B. F. Hepler and B. F. Gardner. He helped establish the First National Bank, and later, the Bank of Fort Scott; he shouldered largely the responsibility in the erection of the Water Works and Sugar works, and has built his share of the fine business houses in the city.

Mr. Drake is a man of much more than average financial ability, and his life might well be taken as a model by any young business man.

AFTER THE AMNESTY.

In the latter part of June, 1858, Capt. Nathaniel Lyon, then in command of the United States troops at Fort Scott, wrote to Governor Denver that:—

"The agreement made by the people here on the occasion of your late visit has been entered upon in good faith, and to this time fully observed."

The newly appointed Sheriff, T. R. Roberts, at once commenced active work against the horse-thieves, especially the gang running with our old acquaintance "Rev." J. E. Stewart, who had again returned. This man Stewart and his men had rendezvous on the Osage and on Drywood, and were sheltered and protected quite as often by men claiming to belong to one side as the other.

A considerable number of horses and other stock stolen by organized bands of theives, were recovered during the summer and returned to their owners by Sheriff Roberts. The Fort Scott *Democrat* of date of July 8th, has this to say: "Sheriff Roberts has recovered nearly all the horses stolen by Rev. J. E. Stewart."

One day Sheriff Roberts and his posse were out to arrest some men who had been with Stewart the spring before, and who had now slipped back again. Rube Forbes was one of them, and he was one of the men Roberts wanted. Dave Forbes, a brother of Rube, was along with the posse. When they got up near Mapleton, they met Rube, or saw him at some little distance in the road. They all knew him at once. Rube knew them also, and fixed himself for a run by throwing away everything loose and tucking his Sharp's rifle down under his leg. Dave, as soon as he saw him, rushed his horse in front of the posse and shouted to Rube to run. Then facing the posse and raising his revolver, he said: "Gentlemen, that man is my brother; the first man that attempts to shoot him is a dead man." And he held that posse until Rube had time to get away.

Soon after peace was restored, Geo. A. Crawford made a trip to Washington to effect the removal of Geo. W. Clark, who had been so long in the Land Office. This he succeeded in doing, although Clark was the pet of somebody near the Administration, who immediately secured for him a fat appointment in the U. S. Navy. But this section of country was rid of him for all time.

G. W. Clark was at heart a bad man. His methods were sneaking and underhanded. He held his office under false pretenses and under a false name, the records of the Land office bearing his name as Doak. He planned and instigated more devilment among his class of rabid Pro-slavery men than any other man on the border. He was not in the Marais des Cygnes murder, but he was in the secret council that planned it in the "dark recesses" of the Western Hotel. Had he and his friends then in Fort Scott ever obtained what they thought to be a sufficient advantage, their first stroke would have fallen on Crawford, Gallaher, Dimon, McDonald, Campbell, Tallman and others, instead of the wholly unprotected and unwary men who formed that fated line on the banks of the Marais des Cygnes.

IMPROVEMENTS CONTINUE.

During the summer the work of improvement went on satisfactorily. Hill & Riggins and Wilson, Gordon

& Ray erected their new stores on Market street and occupied them. The *Democrat* had moved to the second floor of the Town Company's building; the Company occupied the front room, and the post-office the back room of the lower floor. Two Swedes erected the great barn-like building at the Southeast corner of the Plaza, one of them—the big one—packing most of the lumber from the mill on his shoulders, and C. F. Drake occupied the east room for his stove and tin store. William Smith erected a dwelling at the corner of Scott avenue and Locust street. Charley Goodlander put up his shop on the east side of Scott avenue.

EXIT LECOMPTON CONSTITUTION.

Governor Denver had designated the 2nd of August, 1858, as the day for the election on the Lecompton Constitution, as submitted by the provisions of the English Bill.

The election took place on that day, with the following result in Bourbon County:

	Against.	*For.*
Rayville,	53	
Sprattsville,	18	
Mapleton,	84	1
Marmaton,	41	4
Osage,	30	
Mill Creek,	26	
Drywood,	50	13
Fort Scott,	81	19
Total,	383	37

The total vote in the Territory was:

Against the Constitution, ... 11,300
For the Constitution, ... 1,788

Majority against, ... 9,512

And that was the last of the Lecompton Constitution. It was born in iniquity and shame; left in all its squalor on the steps of the White House; there reclothed, a bribe for its adoption hanged around its neck and then returned to the place of its nativity, only to be spurned into a timely grave.

Thus perished the last hope of the incipient Confederacy that they could ever add Kansas to their territory. They gave up the fight. The struggle was over. Kansas was free.

CHAPTER XVIII.

AMNESTY BROKEN.

THE regular election for member of the Territorial Legislature was held on October 4, 1858. Bourbon County was in the 12th District. Thomas R. Roberts was elected the member for this county. On the 10th of October Governor Denver resigned, and Hugh S. Walsh became Acting Governor until the appointment of Samuel Medary, of Ohio. Governor Medary arrived at Lecompton on December 17th and assumed the office of Governor.

The truce agreed to in June had been generally observed and nothing objectionable to any party occurred until in November, when stealing commenced again. The houses of Poyner and Lemons, two farmers living north of Fort Scott, were robbed, and many other depradations were committed. It is not known who committed all these robberies, but they were generally laid onto "Montgomery's men." Some of the robberies were probably committed by men who had, at some time or other, been with Montgomery. There was no "politics" in it more than there would be now days in any plain case of stealing, nor had it anything whatever to do with the amnesty agreement further than a tendency to "stir things up."

About the 17th of November, 1858, a man named Ben Rice, who had figured more or less as a Jayhawker was arrested on old indictments for crimes committed before the amnesty. It was said one indictment was for the murder of old man Travis who had been killed on the Osage nearly a year before. The arrest of Rice, although it was made by a Free State officer, on an indictment found by a grand jury, partly, at least, of Free State men, was regarded by many as a deliberate rupture of the treaty of peace and amnesty, which would be followed by the indictment and arrest of all who had been active in the border difficulties, and that the revival or resumption of the execution of old writs for past offenses of a political nature would fall only on men of the Free State party, as most of the men of the Pro-slavery party who were liable under the law for crimes and misdemeanors had been driven out or had voluntarily left the Territory.

Montgomery also regarded the arrest of Rice on such an indictment as a violation of the agreement with the Governor of June 15th. He argued that all offenses committed prior to that date should be "amnested." The other side claimed that the agreement was, substantially, that for past offences no arrests should be made except on duly authenticated indictments by grand juries. Such in fact was the real spirit and intent of the Denver agreement.

Then followed a couple of weeks of uneasiness and growing dissatisfaction, when a meeting was called at

Rayville to endeavor to quiet things down again. W. R. Griffith was president, J. C. Burnett and Rev. M. Brockman, vice-presidents, and J. E. Jones, secretary.

Montgomery, in a speech interpreted the June agreement, claiming that amnesty was of the essence of that treaty, etc. A motion that offenses committed prior to June 15th be referred to grand juries of the proper counties was lost. On the other hand, a motion to forcibly release Rice was also lost. There was some further discussion, but it was impossible to agree on any line of action, and Montgomery determined on the release of Rice.

RELEASE OF RICE—DEATH OF LITTLE.

On the night of the 15th of December, 1858, a party with the purpose of releasing Ben Rice from custody assembled at the house of old man Wimsett, about three miles west of Fort Scott on the Marmaton river. The leaders present were old John Brown, Montgomery and Jennison. These men had with them their lieutenants and particular followers which they had brought down with them from Linn County, of about fifteen men each. On the Osage they were joined by some twenty more and five or six were added to their force on the way down through the county, making the aggregate number at Wimsett's sixty-eight or seventy men. They also brought down a small cannon, then owned by the Mound City people—now in possession of the State Historical Society—which they called "Betsy." Alec Howard, of Osage, hauled Betsy down in a two-horse wagon.

A general council was then held by the prominent men to arrange details. The question of who should command the expedition came up. Brown wanted to lead. He claimed he was the oldest man and oldest in the border war and should have command. He defined his plan of campaign as the absolute destruction of the town and the killing of all who resisted. Hazlett, Whipple, Kagi and some few others supported Brown. Montgomery claimed that he should lead; that the people of the Osage country, in both counties looked to him and relied on him, and he knew their wishes; that he had been their representative in the Denver agreement, and in all the public meetings at Rayville and other points; that the sole and only object of the expedition was the release of Rice, and that not a single house should be burned or a man killed, and finally, in the most arbitrary manner he declared that he was and would continue in command. Jennison had nothing to say. He was there to go in with anybody and run his chances. He afterwards, in a published "sketch of his life" claimed that he was the leader, but his leadership began after the store was broken open and the goods in sight. The party then started for Fort Scott, crossing the Marmaton at the California ford. Brown remained at Wimsett's. The affair had assumed too insignificant proportions for the great "Liberator" to fool with, especially if he couldn't boss the job.

After their arrival at the edge of town, at the house of J. N. Roach, called "Fort Roach" by the boys, which was a log house near the present corner of National avenue and First street, they halted and there formed into three squads of twenty men each. It was now just daylight, between six and seven o'clock. On reaching the Free State Hotel, where they had previously ascertained Rice was kept, the first division passed quietly by the right to the rear of the house, the second squad to the left, and the third mounted the big flight of stairs in front and passed on up to the third story, where they found Rice and quickly released him. While this was going on a tragedy was being enacted in the building just across the alley from the hotel. This building, still standing, was built by the Government for quartermaster's stores. It is a long, one-story frame house, and was at this time occupied by Little & Son as a general store. A partition had been run through lengthwise, and the part next to the hotel was the storeroom, and the other part was occupied by the Little family. The store had a front entrance and also a side door. John Little and George A. Crawford, for that night, were sleeping in the store. The noise made by the rescuing party aroused their attention. Just then they heard some one cry "Jayhawkers!" Then Little grabbed his gun, opened the front door a few inches and, seeing an armed mob, fired on them, lodging a load of duck-shot in the heavy overcoat worn by Hazlett. Kagi, standing near Hazlett, instantly fired at the door, putting a ball through it just above Little's head. Little then locked the front door and went to the side door, placed a goods box against it and mounted it in order to see through the transom what was going on. The glass in the window was dusty and he took his white handkerchief and was cleaning a spot so he could see out better, when Capt. Whipple, standing about at the corner of the hotel, seeing the handkerchief moving, fired at it with his Sharp's rifle. The bullet struck Little in the forehead, and he dropped to the floor and expired in a few minutes. Then the uproar commenced. The Jayhawkers thought there were armed men in the store. The cannon was brought up to bear on the house. Some one shouted that there were women and children in the house. Then the doors were all opened or broken down, front and rear. They found no one in the front part of the store but Mr. Crawford and the dying Little. They assisted Mr. Crawford in carrying Mr. Little around to the part of the house in which the family lived.

In the meantime several citizens had made their appearance, and as fast as they did so they were arrested. Colonel and Mrs. Wilson, in the next house to the hotel, came out on the porch and were ordered down on the sidewalk among the other prisoners. Alec McDonald, living in the next house to Colonel Wilson's, came out. Jennison, standing on the sidewalk in front of Wilson's, ordered him to surrender and come down there. McDonald declined the invitation and darted inside the door just as Jennison let go at him with his rifle. The ball is in the door now.

Montgomery, seeing Mrs. Wilson, thought he saw in her face a resemblance to Dr. Hogan, who had once befriended him when they all lived in Missouri. On ascertaining that Dr. Hogan was her brother, he at once released her and the Colonel and promised that their store should not be disturbed, but "requested" that the Colonel furnish some of his men with breakfast. The Colonel ordered breakfast at the Western Hotel for thirty, but the men did not stay to eat it.

The jayhawkers on breaking open Little's store, seeing the dry goods, boots, saddles, etc., began to help themselves. Jennison was in there. He took one of the new saddles, turned it over on the floor and piled dry goods and things on it, then buckled the surcingle over them, poked his gun through the bundle, shouldered it and walked off. He looked liked the cuts in newspapers and hand-bills of those days advertising slaves.

C. F. Drake, Crawford and others went to Montgomery and tried to have him stop the stealing. He did try to, but the fellows had got a taste and he could not control them. He did, however, succeed, like in time of a big fire, in "confining it to one block."

Little made a fatal mistake in firing the first shot into the mob. While it cannot be stated without question that if there had been no resistance or show of arms there would have been no bloodshed or firing on unarmed citizens by the rescuing party, it is altogether probable that such would have been the case. There was a bad element along, headed by Jennison, who only awaited an excuse like being first fired on to shoot at any body they saw, or commit any depredation.

George Stockmyer, Mr. Tabor and Mr. Johnson, living in the neighborhood of Dayton, learned of the proposed attempt to release Rice the day before, and with a view of preventing probable trouble, started that night for Fort Scott with the intention of informing the proper officers and getting them to release Rice in advance of the mob. But they were prevented for some reason, and did not get in until too late.

The tragic death of John H. Little was much regretted by all who knew him, not only in town, but throughout the country where he was well acquainted. Every body knew "Little & Son," and Little's Store. He was a man of strong Pro-slavery prejudices, but of late he had nothing to do with politics, but was attending strictly to the business affairs of the store.

The right name of the man who shot Little was Aaron D. Stevens, who was then going under the assumed name of "Capt. Whipple." He had a singular history. At the age of fifteen he went into the Mexican war and, young as he was, he distinguished himself for undaunted courage. After the war his command started home across the plains. One day an officer was grossly abusing a private soldier. Whipple witnessed it as long as he could stand it and then turned in and whaled the officer nearly to death. For that Whipple was sent to Leavenworth, tried, and sentenced to be shot. But he escaped. In January, 1856, he turned up at Topeka, got in with the boys, and was made Captain. Later he joined John Brown and died with him for the Harper's Ferry business, as did also the men called Kagi and Hazlett.

CHAPTER XIX.

MILITIA ORGANIZED.

THE incidents which had occurred during the last of December renewed the excitement throughout the county. The citizens of Fort Scott and the neighborhood made application to Governor Medary for troops. The Governor having no troops to send advised the organization of home militia to act with the Marshal in enforcing the law. They acted on his suggestion and the organization of militia companies was begun about the first of the year. John Hamilton, the old sergeant of the regular army, who was here when the post was established in 1842, was captain of the first company, and C. F. Drake lieutenant. Another company was organized by Alex. McDonald, W. T. Campbell, A. R. Allison and W. C. Denison. Two or three other companies were started; they had plenty of men for officers, but they ran out of men for privates. They finally concluded that, as the weather was pretty cold anyway, they would let old John Hamilton run the military department. Being an old soldier he immediately brought matters into military shape, with roll-call, guard mounting, drill, etc. Their arms were all private property and were of as heterogeneous a character as could well be imagined—flint-lock muskets, rifles of every imaginable pattern, shot-guns, carbines and pistols.

On application of Governor Medary a quantity of smooth-bore muskets were sent to the end of the Pacific railroad, whence, during the month of January, 1859, they were escorted to Paris by a company from Linn County. On the trip, Captain Weaver, in charge of the party, in drawing a loaded gun from a wagon, was accidentally shot and killed.

The greater part of the month of January was spent in drilling. The force was divided into three companies under Captains Hamilton, McDonald and Campbell. J. E. Jones, A. McDonald and W. T. Campbell were appointed Deputy U. S. Marshals. The men were all regularly mustered and sworn in.

Sunday morning, January 30, 1859, a company of fifty men started for Paris after the new arms. The trip occupied four days and on their return preparations were at once made to go in pursuit of the Jayhawkers. The entire mounted force marched at midnight on the 4th of February. Hamilton's company reached the Little Osage, near the present Fort Lincoln, at daybreak.

For three days they scoured the Little Osage country clear to its head, riding almost continuously, and returned to Fort Scott at midnight of the 7th with about a dozen prisoners, completely worn out.

After a few days' rest they proceeded with their prisoners to Lawrence, where they were to be tried.

The difficulties in Southeastern Kansas early engaged the attention of the Legislature, to whom the Governor had presented his version of the matter. To remedy the evils in this part of the Territory the jurisdiction of Douglas county was extended over the infected district, and all persons were ordered to be brought to Lawrence for trial, away from the scene of strife. That is the reason these prisoners are being taken there.

LAWRENCE AND FORT SCOTT GET ACQUAINTED.

Continuing their journey they camped at Black Jack on the night of the 14th. Next morning, at the Wakarusa, Marshal Campbell met them with the news of the passage of the "Amnesty Act," and the captives were turned loose. The wagons and most of the men at once set out on their return to Fort Scott. Some, desirous of visiting Lawrence, since they were so near, and with no suspicion of the reception they would receive, rode on. As they quietly pursued their way up Massachusetts street, and had almost reached the Eldridge House, the cry was raised in the crowd that Hamilton, their Captain, was the Hamilton of Marais des Cygnes fame. In a moment they were beset by a fierce mob numbering several hundred. Resistance was useless. Putting spurs to their horses they dashed for the prairie. But the mob was ahead of them. As they galloped down New Hampshire street they received a perfect avalanche of bullets, brick-bats, rocks, mud and sticks. In a short time they were completely hemmed in, and then there was nothing for it but to surrender. But everything was explained after awhile and they were treated with the greatest consideration during the remainder of their stay in that city.

One good result of this affair was that Lawrence and Fort Scott became better acquainted, and the bad impressions and prejudices of both towns which had existed against each other were, to a great extent, removed. Fort Scott's opinion of Lawrence was that it consisted principally of jayhawkers and thieves, and Lawrence was entirely certain that Fort Scott contained nothing but Border Ruffians, with Doc Hamilton as Mayor and Brockett as Police Judge. When they found that the Fort Scott people were, like the best men of their own town, only interested in the peace and prosperity of Kansas, they felt most kindly towards them, and from that day both communities drew a clearer line between "jayhawkers" and good citizens.

The "Amnesty Act" mentioned was passed by the Legislature only a short time before, and was to this effect:

SEC. 1. That no criminal offenses heretofore committed in the counties of Lykins, Linn, Bourbon, McGee, Allen and Anderson, growing out of any political difference of opinion, shall be subject to any prosecution on complaint or indictment in any court whatsoever in this Territory.

"SEC. 2. That all actions now commenced growing out of political differences of opinion, shall be dismissed."

This act, taking effect immediately after its passage, pardoned and liberated all political prisoners then in custody within the designated limits.

COUNTY SEAT MOVED.

In the winter of 1859 the county seat was moved from

Fort Scott to Marmaton City. There was a combination of circumstances which effected this removal. There was a feeling that the records and other property of the county would be more secure away from Fort Scott. There was also considerable feeling of animosity against that town, as the result of old prejudices, and it is probable, also, that a scheme for a real estate speculation, headed by T. R. Roberts, the Representative in the Legislature, had something to do with it. At any rate the records were moved, and the first meeting of the County Board was held on the 25th day of February, 1859. At this meeting the townships of Freedom, Franklin and Marmaton were organized.

The people of Fort Scott sat still and saw the records and offices moved away without much protest, as they, even then, relied on their "natural advantages" for the future of their town. But C. F. Drake and a few others realized the necessity for having the County Seat at Fort Scott, if it was in future to be the principal town in the county, and they went to work to recover it, as will be seen hereafter.

PREPARING FOR ANOTHER CONSTITUTION.

On the 7th of March, 1859, Governor Medary issued a proclamation calling an election for or against holding a Constitutional Convention, in order to ascertain whether or not the people wished a State government.

This election was held on the 28th of March, 1859. It was the first step under the movement for the Wyandotte Constitution.

Bourbon County voted as follows:

For a Constitutional Convention. 333
Against a Constitutional Convention 47

Majority for 286

The total vote in the Territory was:
For a Constitutional Convention 5,306
Against 1,425

Majority for 3,881

This was a very light vote. There was but little division of public sentiment on the question, and no contest at the polls. Everybody was in favor of a State government, except a few bad smelling politicians, old time Jayhawkers and Border Ruffians, whose "political principles" had degenerated into the sole desire to see the country kept embroiled and the field kept open for plundering, thieving and guerrilla warfare.

AN ALL-AROUND GOOD YEAR.

The spring of 1859 opened and continued fairly seasonable, except there was a little too much rain. Even up to June the rivers and streams, from the Marais des Cygnes down, were often past fording, and sometimes out of their banks. But, nevertheless, the prospect for growing crops was good, and there had been much more planting than ever before.

Emigrants were coming into the Territory in large numbers, although that year the "Pike's Peak" excitement was at its height, which diverted much the larger stream of emigration to the gold fields of the Rocky Mountains.

Bourbon County, however, in spite of the troubles, trials and vexations she had passed through, in spite of the marauding of irresponsible men, which had cast an odium on her good name, and in spite of the heretofore almost lawless condition of society, was, nevertheless, receiving a fair share of good farmers and good men. The valleys of the Osage, Marmaton and Drywood were filling up, and the high open prairie was being intruded upon by the cabin and corral. Towns were springing up,—Dayton, Xenia, Uniontown, Rockford, Cato,—all with at least a store, and a post office.

The names of all who settled in the county that year should be recorded here, but it is impossible. They came in too thick.

Fort Scott received a good increase in population during 1859, also. Among the many coming in that year was C. W. Blair.

Charles W. Blair located in Fort Scott in the spring of 1859. He was born in Georgetown, Ohio, February 5, 1829. He studied law when a youth and at the age of twenty-one was Prosecuting Attorney for his county. December 25, 1858, he was married to Miss Katherine Medary, daughter of Hon. Samuel Medary, who was soon afterwards appointed Governor of Kansas Territory. He was accompanied to Fort Scott by his old law tutor, Hon. Andrew Ellison, and they entered immediately upon the practice of law, which has been the occupation of his life except the interim during the late war. Blair was always a Free State Democrat, and after Sumpter was fired on he was a War Democrat in the full sense of the term. He began his war service by raising the first company of soldiers organized in Fort Scott. Afterwards, he passed through the several grades of Major, Lieutenant-Colonel and Colonel, and in the latter part of the war was promoted Brigadier General, at the special request of U. S. Grant. His star was, in part, gained on the bloody ridge of Wilson Creek, when, after the incompetent "political General" Sigel was crushed and his guns taken, and he discovered he was fighting Americans, the rebel host turned in full force on the main line—when, after the noble Mitchell and Deitzler, of the First and Second Kansas, had fallen badly wounded, Lieutenant-Colonel Blair took command of both those stunned and shattered regiments, rallied them into line on the right of the Iowa men and advanced to the ringing call of Lyon: "Come on, brave men, I will lead you."

CHAPTER XX.

DELEGATES TO THE WYANDOTTE CONVENTION.

THE election of delegates to the Wyandotte Constitutional Convention occurred on the 4th of June. The candidates for delegates from Bourbon County were J. C. Burnett and W. R. Griffith, Republicans, and Ezra Gilbert and Hugh Glen, Democrats. The election resulted as follows:

J. C. Burnett,	281
W. R. Griffith,	294
Ezra Gilbert,	229
Hugh Glen,	229

In the Territory 14,000 votes were cast. The Republicans elected 35 and the Democrats 17 delegates. The Convention was to meet at Wyandotte on the 5th of July, 1859.

Affairs in Bourbon County were now quiet. Peace had apparently come to stay. As the 4th of July approached the people decided to celebrate in the good old-fashioned way. Meetings were held, committees appointed and all the preliminary arrangements made. They proposed to invite everybody to come and participate, and give them a good dinner. The preparations were on an enormous scale. There were loads of cooked beef, pork and mutton, mountains of bread; immense quantities of cake and pie, prepared by the ladies. A four-horse wagon load of ice was brought from the Marais des Cygnes at a cost of 10 cents per pound, for manufacture of lemonade. The ground selected was in the bottom, just west of the point of the bluff back of town, near the big spring. Governor Ransom was President of the Day; Hon. Jos. Williams, Colonel Judson, Judge Farwell, M. E. Hudson, Thomas Helm, W. T. Campbell and Colonel Morin, Vice-presidents; Rev. Mr. Thompson, Chaplain; Mason Williams, Reader; L. A. McCord, Orator.

The crowd was immense; the usual proceedings were had; all were filled, some of them apparently for a month ahead.

A GRAND BALL.

In the evening there was a "grand ball" at the Fort Scott Hotel. Again Joe Ray "called," assisted by C. W. Goodlander. The boys were supplied with "invitations" printed on small sheets of note paper, with display type and gold-tinted letters, gotten up in the very best style of the job office.

The boys would take these "ball tickets," fill in the name of their "first choice," and in the event that she was already engaged or couldn't go, would fill out another invitation and send to some other girl. Keep trying.

The colored people had a ball that same night, just in the rear of the hotel. They didn't have to go to the expense of music or the trouble of "calling." They just waited till the white folks started up, and then went at it with a whoop.

THE FORT SCOTT "DEMOCRAT" REVIVED.

Sometime before this, J. E. Jones had suspended the publication of the *Democrat*, and left town. The Town Company, who owned the material, was desirous that the paper should be revived, so negotiations with that end in view, were opened with William Smith and his son, E. A. Smith, who decided to give it a trial. The first number under their management was issued on the 14th of July, 1859, and they continued its publication regularly until the summer of 1861, some time after the breaking out of the war, when E. A. Smith left the editorial chair and went into the army.

In 1882 he published in one of the city papers a considerable amount of excerpts from the *Democrat*, something in the diary form, which he said "was not designed as a connected narative or history, but rather as data which may aid some one else in such a work." These data were principally in reference to events which occurred in Fort Scott, and were of great assistance in the preparation of this work, especially in the matter of dates.

The advertising columns of the first number of the *Democrat* show at that time a very respectable business community. Of lawyers there were Ellison & Blair, William Margrave, S. A. Williams, John C. Sims, C. P. Bullock, Richard Stadden, Williams & Bro. (Mason and Wm. M.,) James J. Farley, George A. Crawford, and L. A. McCord; there were doctors J. H. Couch, A. M. H. Bills, and A. G. Osbun. E. A. Smith was County Surveyor. General merchandise was represented by H. T. Wilson, Hill & Riggins, George A. Crawford & Co.

John S. Caulkins was in the clothing, Malone in the grocery, and C. F. Drake in the stove and tinware business. Then there were Robert Blackett and Daniel Funk, tailors; C. W. Goodlander and Dennison & Waterhouse, carpenters; John G. Stuart, carriage and wagon maker; E. L. Marble, boot and shoemaker; Tom Huston, saddle and harnessmaker; Fort Scott Hotel, B. B. Dillon, prop.; Western Hotel, Linn & Harris, props.; Harry Hartman, bakery and ice cream saloon.

WYANDOTTE CONSTITUTION.

The Wyandotte convention completed their labors on the 4th day of October, 1859.

The vote in the Territory was as follows:
For the Constitution 10,421
Against 5,530

The vote in Bourbon County was:
For the Constitution 464
Against 256

This was the Constitution under which the Territory was finally admitted into the Union as a State.

On the 8th of November an election was held for delegate to Congress, and for Territorial Legislature.

In Bourbon County the vote was as follows: For Delegate, M. J. Parrott, Republican, 368; S. W. Johnson, Democrat, 251. For Representative, H. Knowles, Republican, 359; G. Hubbard, Democrat, 259.

On the 6th day of December an election was had under the Wyandotte Constitution for State officers,

Representative in Congress and State Legislature, to take effect when the Territory should be admitted as a State. Charles Robinson was the Republican and Samuel Medary the Democratic candidate for Governor, Martin F. Conway, Republican, and J. A. Halderman, Democrat, for Congress; W. R. Griffith of Bourbon County was the Republican candidate for Superintendent of Public Instruction. The entire Republican State ticket was elected by about 7,900, against 5,400. The vote in Bourbon County on Governor—and about the same on the other officers—was: Robinson, 275; Medary, 149. J. C. Burnett, Republican, was elected for State Senator by 270, against Geo. A. Crawford, Democrat, 141. Horatio Knowles was elected Representative by the same vote.

A District Judge was also elected December 6th, under the Wyandotte Constitution. Bourbon County was to be in the Fourth District with Allen, Anderson, Douglas, Franklin, Johnson, Linn and Lykins, (afterwards Miami). Solon O. Thatcher, Republican, and James Christian, Democrat, were the candidates. The vote in this county was substantially the same as for Governor, and Solon O. Thatcher became our first District Judge.

Judge Thatcher served until 1864 when he resigned, and Hon. D. P. Lowe, then of Linn County, was appointed to fill the vacancy.

Epaphroditus Ransom died at his residence in Fort Scott, Nov. 11th. B. B. Dillon died on the 16th.

Mr. Rankin organized a Presbyterian church in Fort Scott. It was composed of John S. Caulkins, Mrs. A. McDonald and Mrs. Wm. Smith.

NEAR BANDERA ON THE MARMATON.

Residence, near Marmaton, of W. R. Griffith, First State Supt. of Public Instruction. 1861.

CHAPTER XXI.

LEGISLATURE MEETS.

THE Territorial Legislature met at Lecompton on the 2d of January, 1860, but soon after adjourned to Lawrence. The town of Dayton was incorporated by an act of this Legislature, approved February 18, 1860. The Dayton Town Company consisted of George Stockmyer, D. J. Patterson, E. Kepley, George A. Crawford, O. Darling, C. E. Cranston, J. S. Dejernett and Amos Stewart.

FORT SCOTT TOWN COMPANY INCORPORATED.

On the 27th of February, 1860, the Legislature passed an act incorporating the Fort Scott Town Company. The company had been in existence since January, 1857, but had not up to this time been incorporated by law. Geo. A. Crawford, W. R. Judson, Joseph Williams, E. S. Lowman, H. T. Wilson and Norman Eddy were named in the act of incorporation.

FORT SCOTT INCORPORATED AS A CITY.

On this same date—February 27, 1860—an act was passed with the following title:

"An act to amend an act to incorporate the town of Fort Scott." Section First provided:

"That all that district of land described as follows, to-wit:—The southwest quarter, the west half of the southeast quarter, the southwest quarter of the northeast quarter and the southeast quarter of the northwest quarter of Section Thirty, Township Twenty-five, of Range Twenty-five, be and hereby is declared to be a city by the name and style of the City of Fort Scott."

The act also provided that the first election should take place on the second Monday of March, 1860. A. R. Allison, S. A. Williams and C. F. Drake were named inspectors of said election.

FIRST CITY ELECTION—COUNTY ELECTION.

The city election took place according to law, and resulted in the choice of the following officers: Mayor, W. R. Judson; Councilmen, H. T. Wilson, C. W. Blair, John S. Redfield and George A. Crawford; Clerk, Wm. Gallaher; Recorder, Wm. Margrave; Marshal, Richard Phillips; Assessor, John S. Caulkins; Treasurer, A. McDonald; Street Commissioner, A. R. Allison. At this election, the first in the new city, 81 votes were cast. W. R. Judson failed to qualify as Mayor, and Joseph Ray was elected to that position, and became the first Mayor of Fort Scott.

On the 10th of September, 1860, Joseph Ray, as Mayor, purchased the town-site of Fort Scott from the United States, consisting of 319 11-100 acres, as described in the act of February 27th, incorporating it as a City. The patent afterwards issued by the Government for the land described is dated July 10, 1861.

About the 1st of April, 1860, a county election was held at which the following named county officers were chosen : County Commissioners, Isaac Ford, Lester Ray, G. W. Miller; Probate Judge, H. Knowles; Assessor, J. N. Roach; Treasurer, J. Aitkin; Register of Deeds, W. H. Norway; Coroner, Dr. Freeman.

THE LAST BORDER DIFFICULTIES.

In May, 1860, the notorious "Pickles" of Linn County, a general all-round thief, was arrested and brought to Fort Scott for trial for theft. His real name was Wright, but he got his nick-name of "Pickles" for having, in one of his expeditions, stolen a two-quart jar of pickles and devoured them as he rode along. When taken into court he plead guilty to the charge of horse-stealing, and was at once sentenced to the penitentiary, as an act of discretion, to avoid falling into the hands of an Osage Vigilance Committee, who had assembled in town, headed by old Billy Baker with a rope. Some of Pickles' gang came down as far as the Osage and endeavored to raise a rescuing party, after the Ben Rice fashion, but they soon abandoned the project. The day for that sort of thing had passed. The vigilance committee mentioned, or anti-horse thief society, as they called themselves, which had been formed up about Mapleton, came into town to look after the Pickles trial, with an eye open for a possible attempt at rescue.

Pickles fared better than did a man named Guthrie, who, some time before this, was found with a horse supposed not to belong to him, and was taken from the hands of a constable and hanged by this committee. They also got hold of Hugh Carlin, who had given the settlers on the Osage a good deal of trouble, and in the early part of July he was taken from the house of A. F. Monroe, without giving him time to dress, and that was the last of Hugh Carlin.

In these hangings a young man named L. D. Moore was particularly active as a member of the committee. On the night of the 16th of November he was visited by Jennison, with a squad of about twenty men. Upon arriving at Moore's house, Jennison kicked open the door and shot Moore before he had time to get out of bed. This murder was in retaliation for the hanging of Carlin. Although Moore, who had settled on the Osage in 1857, was a Pro-slavery man, politics had little or nothing to do with his death. It was a kind of an afterthought—a finishing up job of Jennison's, who two days before that had started out on a circuit in Linn county, first hanging old man Scott in his own door yard, in the north part of that county; the next day hanging Rus Hines near the Missouri State line, east of Mine creek, and winding up with the killing of Moore. The first two were killed on the pretext that they had aided in the return to the owners of runaway negroes, and Moore was killed because he was, as Jennison said, "a little too —— conservative."

There was, in the fall of 1860, a secret society organized in Linn county, which they called the "Wide

Awakes." It probably existed to a more or less extent all along the border. In Linn county it was especially strong. Nearly every Free State man in that county joined it. The fundamental principles of this society were opposition to the enforcement of the Fugitive Slave Law; to take measures on all occasions to nullify its provisions; to uphold the officers, sheriffs, etc., in its nullification; to forcibly prevent the return of fugitive slaves, and, when they got over into Kansas, to give them a bag full of grub and show them the north star. The society did not, however, propose to take violent measures in the case of men who were aiding and assisting in the execution of the law. But Jennison and a few with him took the general feeling as a license for him to do so, and the death of Scott and Hines, and indirectly that of Moore, was the result.

In Bourbon County all these murders, by both parties, caused a decided revulsion of feeling, not only against the Jayhawkers, but all other species of mob violence, vigilance committees, protective societies, etc., in all forms. The point was passed where anything more of that kind would be tolerated. The disposition and determination of the public mind was to inaugarate LAW, to establish the forms and precedents they had been accustomed to in the old States, and thus bring order out of the utter chaos which had so far reigned from the day the Territory was organized. It was not hoped that this could be accomplished in a day, but it was, nevertheless, practically so, for these were the last outrages perpetrated under the guise of "Free State" or "Pro-slavery."

CHAPTER XXII.

THE ARTS OF PEACE.

THE idea of improving their homes, establishing schools amd churches, instituting county fairs, building railways, etc., began to take possession of the people. Hardly a week passed that there was not an enthusiastic meeting in the interest of some line. Among the proposed roads were the "Tebo and Neosho," afterwards the Missouri, Kansas and Texas, the "Fort Scott, Neosho and Santa Fe." and the "Lake Superior, Fort Scott and Galveston." There was some talk of the "Hudson's Bay, Fort Scott and Honduras," but they considered that it would be too nearly a parallel line and would interfere with the business and carrying trade of the Lake Superior, Fort Scott and Galveston route, so that project was dropped.

The question of an Agricultural Society, County Fair, etc., received due attention. At a meeting held at Marmaton on the 14th of June, at which A. G. Osbun was President, and W. R. Griffith, Secretary, it was resolved to form an association to be known as "The Bourbon County Agricultural Society." J. M. Liggitt, A. Decker, and Judge Farwell were appointed a committee to draft a constitution and report at the next meeting.

At the next meeting the Bourbon County Agricultural Society was fully organized by the election of the following officers: President, Dr. A. G. Osbun; Vice-President, Richard Stadden; Secretary, Wm. R. Griffith; Treasurer, Isaac N. Mills; Executive Committee, H. C. Moore, Aaron Decker, Ezekiel Brown, Harrison Martin and S. B. Farwell. The first annual exhibition was to be held at the residence of Mr. Griffith, near Marmaton, on the 24th and 25th of October.

The Fair was held according to programme, and was better than could have been expected under the circumstances. There had been no rain for a year, but they did the best they could. They were a little short on big pumpkins and long corn, but the show of live stock and fancy work was very good.

POPULATION—N. Y. INDIAN LANDS.

During the spring of 1860, Will Gallaher took the census of this part of the Territory, and returned the following statistics: Number of inhabitants in Bourbon County, 6,102; deaths during the year ending June 1, 1860, 101; mills and manufacturing establishments, 9; farmers, 1,200. Inhabitants on the Cherokee Neutral Lands, 2,025.

As was stated in the first part of this book, the number of Indian claims allowed on the New York lands was thirty-two, equal to 10,240 acres. This tract had been located in the neighborhood of Barnesville. The residue of the tract, comprising a million acres of the best land in Kansas, was turned over to the General Land Office as public land, subject to entry and sale, about the 20th of June, 1860. The plats were at the Land Office in Fort Scott, and settlers commenced filing and pre-empting.

In reference to those thirty-two allotments, in several instances the occupying Indians were driven off at the time the Free State men in the same locality were driven out in 1856, and some of them never returned. Their lands were taken possession of by white settlers, who were afterwards permitted to acquire title from the Goverment. The Indians so driven off afterwards applied to the Court of Claims for compensation, and their claims were allowed thirty years later.

ON THE NEUTRAL LANDS.

By this time a large number of settlers had gone onto the Cherokee Neutral Land, squatted on claims, built cabins and made other improvements. They were trespassers by law and by treaty stipulations, but they claimed the usual pioneers equity in Indian lands, and had the moral support, at least, of all the other settlers.

On October 27, 1860, the agent of the Cherokees, with a body of troops, commenced the work of driving all the settlers off the Neutral Land. Orders to that end were issued by the Commissioners of General Land Office in the spring, but on a representation of the facts temporarily suspended. The present move was entirely unexpected. From 75 to 100 houses were burned, and as many families rendered destitute. These were in outlying settlements. When the agent reached Drywood he found the settlers united and determined, and concluded to give them one month's grace. There was not a Cherokee on the land, and, moreover, there was no desire on the part of the Indians that the whites should be disturbed.

Delegations were sent to Washington by the business men of Fort Scott in the interest of the settlers on the Neutral Lands in Bourbon County. Colonel Wilson, who was familiar with the Cherokee people, went to Tahlequa to ascertain the feeling of the head men in reference to a sale of the Neutral Land. But the matter was not quite ripe. In several instances the settlers on the Neutral Land married Cherokee women, thereby becoming "squawmen"—legally Cherokees—and entitled to a "headright," and thus securing their claims. Old man Hathaway, on Drywood, was one instance in this county.

As has been noted, there was a very large immigration into this county during the winter and spring of 1860, "too numerous to mention." Among the many who came to Fort Scott that spring must be noted the arrival of John S. Miller and family on the 5th of March. Mr. Miller was from Pennsylvania, of the old "Pennsylvania Dutch" stock, and was a most excellent man and citizen. He was active in business circles, and in the affairs of the city, township and county.

ARRIVAL OF TROOPS.

About the 1st of December, 1860, General Harney

and staff arrived. The command came the next day. It numbered about 180 men. The officers were Brigadier General Harney, Captain Jones, A. A. G.; Lieutenant Armstrong, Aid; Lieutenant Tidball, A. A. Q. M.; Swift and Brewer, Surgeons; Lieutenant Mullins, 1st Dragoons; Captain Barry and Lieutenants Fry, Bargar, Sullivan and Perry of the artillery.

The Jennison "circuit" detailed some pages back, had occasioned a great scare, and the troops came here for the purpose of protecting the border. The Governor of Missouri had also sent a brigade of Missouri militia to the State line under command of Gen. D. M. Frost, afterwards of the rebel army, and of "Camp Jackson" fame. One purpose of having troops at Fort Scott was to be present at the land sales which occurred on the 3d of December, 1860. Only fourteen 80-acre tracts were disposed of, at prices ranging from $1.25 to 5.50 per acre. The attendance was very large. The lands were all offered by 12 o'clock, and the people went home satisfied their claims were safe for another year.

THE GREAT DROUTH.

The year 1860 is known as the "dry year." The long drouth really commenced in the latter part of 1859. The year 1859 up to August or September was very seasonable. Crops were all made and the yield was immense. It was most fortunate they were so, for the crops of 1859 saved the people in the next year. Corn turned out from sixty to ninety bushels to the acre. Even sod corn made an immense yield.

The Fort Scott *Democrat* of November 10, 1859, is the authority for the statement that "Mr. Buckner, living between Marmaton and Mill Creek, this season raised six hundred bushels of corn on seven acres of sod." Wheat and oats were good. Prairie grass grew to a height of from three to four feet.

The immigrants coming in that spring and summer, seeing the rich overflow of a bounteous harvest, and the summertide of glorious verdure, hearing on every side the gurgling springs and brooks as they trilled in limpid silver down the ravines, thought that this was in truth the Elysian fields, the abode of the blest, and they felt like sending up their voices in grand diapason of the vox humana. If such was the natural condition, they thought, if vegetation existed in such luxuriance, if every "draw" contained a spring and every ravine was a creek, it certainly surpassed any country of which they had ever dreamed.

But the scene was to change.

About the 1st day of September, 1859, it quit raining. The 1st of January, 1860, came, but still no rain or "falling weather." The winter crept along, not very cold but very dry. Spring came, and still no rain. The farmer plowed as usual for crops, which were planted at the usual time, but no rain yet. Corn and other crops sprouted and came up, but no showers gladdened the tender shoots. The wind blew incessantly from the southwest. Occasionally a cloud would come over about the size of a ten-acre lot, and it would sprinkle a little. Sometimes a bank of clouds would loom up in the northwest in the evening, shake their

heads and disappear. On the 16th of June a thunder
shower came up, and it lightened and thundered and
blowed and raged, and it rained—a little; so little that
it was only an aggravation.

Corn made a brave effort to grow. It was pitiful to
look at. It held up its withered blades as if imploring
the brazen heavens to let down rain. The poor, little
spindling stalks grew up about three feet high, tasseled
out, and then died. During the first part of July the
thermometer ranged from 98 to 104 degrees in the
shade. In the sun at midday is was 132°. By the
middle of July the heat was simply awful. It is a
matter of record that on the 13th, and for weeks after
that, the thermometer often went up to 112, 113 and
114 degrees in the shade. There was a wind—almost
a gale sometimes—but it came up, seemingly, with a
spiral twist—hot, scorching, withering, like a blast
from a seething furnace. People sought their houses
and closed the doors and windows to keep it out. The
foliage on the trees withered up and blew off. The
prairie grass, which had grown up about three inches
high, turned brown and was dry enough to burn. It is
said that eggs would roast in the sand at midday—were
actually so roasted. There is no doubt of it. The
thermometer was 146 degrees in the sun. Thus the
terrible drouth continued day after day, week after
week, month after month.

Springs, wells, water everywhere, gave out. The
farmer sought the lowest "draw" on his place and dug
down for water, sometimes with partial success. The
creeks and larger streams were perfectly dry except in

the large "holes," which, ordinarily from ten to fifteen feet in depth, were reduced to muddy, stagnant puddles. There would often be a stretch of a mile or more between these pools in which the bottom of the river was dry and dusty, and the dry leaves, lately fallen from the trees, would rustle and swirl in the little whirlwinds as they swept up and down the river bed.

In the latter part of September or first part of October the drouth was partially broken. It rained a little. The rains were not general or heavy, but it rained enough to freshen up the stagnant pools, and form many small ones. Stock water was not so scarce, and once more the cow and yoke of steers could have enough to drink.

The drouth had lasted for more than a year. Dates of its beginning and ending vary with localities, but it may be said, in general, that there were from twelve to fourteen calendar months during which time the total rainfall did not exceed one inch.

Of course all crops were practically a failure. In fields around the base of the mounds, which in ordinary years are wet and springy, and in some places in the low bottom lands some corn was raised, in some instances as much as five bushels to the acre, of little wormy-ended nubbins. Sorghum sugar cane did better than any other crop. In fact, it made a fair yield where planted, and all that fall the creak of the cane mills could be heard in neighborhoods where they had been fortunate enough to have planted cane.

In the year before, a good crop of cane had been raised on a small patch of ground on the farm of Dr.

A. G. Osbun. In harvesting the cane that fall the seed had rattled out over the ground and in the spring it came up quite a thick "volunteer" crop. It grew that season about four or five feet high, being so thick on the ground, and was cut and put up like hay, and fed to the horses and other stock that winter.

Unfortunately but few farmers in this county had sorghum seed, and but little was planted. In Linn County this crop was quite general and very good. The farmers there made any amount of molasses, but some had nothing to "put it on." Children were often seen eating sorghum molasses off a chip instead of their much loved crust of corn bread.

This general failure of crops of course caused much suffering, especially as winter approached and the store of old corn in the country became more nearly exhausted. Many were compelled to leave the country temporarily, to seek subsistence. In such cases where the family had a claim it was the tacit understanding that their claims should be protected until their return the next year.

Efforts were begun that fall in the direction of securing aid. Delegations were sent East to represent the facts and solicit help. Considerable aid was received in this county, but not as much as in that part of the country contiguous to the Missouri river, up which all freights had to come at that day. From here it was a round trip of two hundred miles to Wyandotte.

There were a few intermittent rains and snows during that fall and winter, but the flood gates were not opened and the streams flushed until early in April, 1861.

CHAPTER XXIII.

KANSAS ADMITTED.

KANSAS was admitted as a State on the 29th day of January, 1861. It came to the fireside of the Union only to witness the frowning and wayward sisters of the South departing, one by one, across the threshold, out into the darkness—out into the coming storm. But Kansas came not in the innocence of childhood, nor like "a fair young girl, with light and delicate limbs and waving tresses," but "like a bearded man; armed to the teeth, one mailed hand grasping the broad shield and one the sword; its brow, glorious though it be, is scarred with tokens of old wars." On its shield was written, Ad Astra per Aspera; on its sword, Excalibur Expurgatorius.

The Territorial probation was at an end. The untried and unexampled task set before it had been accomplished, not as designed by the spirit of the past ages, but as marked out by the advancing rays of the Nineteenth Century.

STATE GOVERNMENT.

The Territorial Legislature adjourned on the 2nd day of February, to meet no more.

Governor Charles Robinson was sworn into office on the 9th day of February, as the first Governor of the State of Kansas. He convened the State Legislature, elected under the Wyandotte Constitution, on the 26th day of March. The members of that Legislature from Bourbon County were: J. C. Burnett, of Mapleton, Senator. Horatio Knowles, of Marmaton, S. B. Mahurin, of Scott, and J. T. Neal, of Osage, were the Representatives. James H. Lane and S. C. Pomeroy were elected United States Senators on the 4th day of April.

CITY AFFAIRS.

The population of the City of Fort Scott was now about 500. At the regular spring election for municipal officers the result was as follows:—Mayor, Joseph Ray; Councilmen, H. T. Wilson, J. S. Redfield, A. McDonald and Chas. W. Blair; Clerk, William Gallaher; Treasurer, C. W. Goodlander; Recorder, J. S. Miller; Assessor, A. R. Allison; Marshal, R. L. Philips; Street Commissioner, J. G. Stuart.

The vote was 83, which indicated about the population of 500, as stated.

IMPENDING CRISIS.

The Southern States had now nearly all seceded and their Provisional Government was in full operation at Montgomery, Alabama.

Still, the people of Bourbon County, in common with the entire North, laid the flattering unction to their souls that in some way, or by some means, the impending war might yet be averted. The Governor of the State had appointed four commissioners to the Peace Convention, two of whom had voted for peace and compromise. Meetings were held in various parts of this county, all of which expressed sentiments of conservatism, and especially a spirit of conciliation towards the people of the neighboring State of Missouri living along our border. The leading Democratic citizens of Fort Scott united with the Republicans in a letter to James H. Lane, inviting him to come down and make a speech. He accepted, and came about the 15th of March, and spoke at a public meeting that day.

The attendance at the meeting was very large, and included many citizens of the adjoining portion of Missouri. Lane advocated the cultivation of amicable relations between the people of the two States. He advised the belligerent portion of the Kansas people to "get a bag of meal under the bed, a ham in the cellar, and a dress for the baby," before engaging in a war which would be certain to desolate and impoverish the whole country.

A few days afterwards—about the 20th—a large and enthusiastic meeting of the citizens of Linn and Bourbon Counties, Kansas, and Vernon County, Missouri, was held at Barnesville. It was presided over by H. G. Moore, Sheriff of Bourbon County. Byron P. Ayres, of Linn County, was secretary. James H. Lane, W. L. Henderson, A. B. Massey, J. T. Neal, Ben Rice, George A. Crawford, Chas. W. Blair, C. W. McDaniel, Geo. A. Reynolds, and A. Burton were appointed a committee on resolutions. The resolutions were conservative throughout. General Lane afterwards addressed the meeting in about the same tenor as in his speech at Fort Scott.

The circumstances attending this meeting,—the congregation of a mass of men who had been so long in a whirling eddy of sectional discord,—the appointment on working committees of men who had heretofore entertained such widely differing opinions,—is worthy of historical note.

The old order of things had passed away. The public mind was adjusting itself on new lines; the political atmosphere was clearing up—clear as a bell, and the bell had but one tone.

WAR.

On the 12th of April, 1861, was fired the first gun of the civil war. By a singular coincidence the deed was performed by an old fellow with whose name we have become quite familiar. It was Ruffian. He was probably not the "Ruffian" of our acquaintance, but his act in pulling the lanyard over that old smoothbore Napoleon gun, which fired the first shot against Fort Sumpter, was the climax of the political doctrine that had been taught, not only to our Border Ruffian, but to the entire people of the South. The firing of that gun was the natural and logical sequence and culmination of that spirit—that political essence— which the people of Kansas had contended against for four long years, and which the Government, and the people of all the other states were to now take up on an appeal, and enter into a gigantic trial of another four year's duration.

The artillery "heard around the world" on that April day opened the greatest conflict the world has ever seen. It was the grandest, most momentous sound ever heard on earth. Artillery is God's own music. The reverberating thunder of artillery, the steady tread of contending hosts—fierce, bloody war—these are God's instruments for the advancement and civilization of the human race, and have been since the days of Joshua.

Every war in every nation,—every war between nations,—cuts through the film of ignorance on the eyes of the people, and advances the banner of regeneration and disenthralment. The real camp followers are freedom, tolerance, invention, science. War breaks the fetters of the serf and the slave; it unyokes the woman from the plow team; it casts off the wooden sabots of the listeners to the Angelus.

THE WAR FEELING IN BOURBON COUNTY.

After the war had actually commenced,—after the first "overt act," as we called it, the conservatism, the doubts, the hesitation, of our people were laid aside, together with their politics. The *Democrat*, the only newspaper in the county, came out early and declared that it abandoned all party affiliations and announced itself "for the constitution and the union, and a supporter of the new Administration so long as it shall labor in the direction of their perpetuity." That was the universal sentiment. If war must come the feeling was not only to prepare for it but to prosecute it to the end. Our people realized, also, more nearly than those of other sections of the North the full import of what was to come. The "Ninety Day" theory of Secretary Seward met with no believers. The opinion was, also, often expressed, that the war would result in the extinction of human slavery on this continent.

On Thursday night, April 24th, there was a Union demonstration, the most enthusiastic yet held in the town. The demonstration was entirely impromptu—nine-tenths of those who took part in it being aroused from their slumbers at midnight. As each one joined the procession he was greeted with three cheers, followed by three times three for the Union. "The Red, White and Blue," "Star Spangled Banner," "Yankee Doodle," "Hail Columbia," and other patriotic airs were sung amid the wildest applause. All party feeling was buried beneath the glorious platform of National Union. It was a scene worthy of our town, and one long to be remembered with feelings of deep emotion by every true and loyal citizen.

At a meeting held in the office of C. W. Blair, Esq., Wednesday evening following, two volunteer companies were organized and the following officers elected: First company—Captain, C. W. Blair; First Lieutenant, A. R. Allison; Second Lieutenant, R. L. Phillips; Third Lieutenant, Chas. Bull; Ensign, Wm. R. Judson. Second company—Captain, A. McDonald; First Lieutenant, Charles Dimon; Second Lieutenant, William Gallaher; Third Lieutenant, A. F. Bicking; Ensign, O. S. Dillon. The officers were elected by the combined vote of both companies, leaving each man to decide afterwards with which company he would connect himself.

There were two companies formed in Drywood township about this same time, under command of Captains Henry Coffman and E. J. Boring, and one company on the head of Lightning Creek officered by John T. McWhirt, Roswell Seeley, John Tully, John F. Gates and Sam McWhirt.

The first two Fort Scott companies were finally consolidated, and called themselves the "Frontier Guard." The boys started for Lawrence to be mustered into the service. At Lawrence Captain Blair was promoted to Lieutenant-Colonel of the 2d Kansas, which was to be the regiment of the Fort Scott company. After a few days rest at Lawrence, the regiment left for Kansas City for muster-in. When they got to Wyandotte, about June 1st, most of the Fort Scott boys concluded they had seen enough service and returned home. The larger part of them, however, went into the army afterwards. "Frontier Guard No. 2" was raised soon afterwards by W. T. Campbell, and a company was raised on Mill Creek by Captain Hall.

All this was the usual preliminary business that occurred at that time all over the country, with the object of not only testing who really wanted to go to war, but who were prepared at short notice to leave home for an indefinite time.

The Fourth of July had now come, and was quite a gala day in Fort Scott. It had been arranged that Fort Scott Guards, Nos. 1 and 2, should have a parade and drill, and several companies from the surrounding country were invited to join them. The company from Drywood (cavalry,) Capt. Boring, and Mill Creek company, (infantry,) Capt. Hall, responded to the invitation.

At 10 a. m. the Guards formed at their respective armories, and after a little marching and countermarching, went out to meet and escort in Captain Boring's company. The field music was excellent. The Drywood boys were received with hearty cheers and escorted into town, where the Mill Creek boys were met and received with like cordiality. After dinner the cavalry was drilled by Captain John Hamilton, and the infantry had a battalion drill under E. A. Smith. At five o'clock the battalion was dismissed, and all parties returned to their homes, mutually pleased with the Fourth of July and each other.

On the 5th day of July the battle of Carthage was fought. This occasioned great alarm and apprehension. We had a war sure enough and it was getting uncomfortably close.

Shortly after the Carthage affair General Lyon authorized Captains W. T. Campbell and W. C. Ransom to raise two companies of one hundred men each, to serve as Home Guards. Then two other companies were raised by Captains Z. Gower and Lewis R. Jewell, and these four companies were the origin and foundation of the Sixth Kansas Cavalry.

CHAPTER XXIV.

BATTLE OF DRYWOOD.

THE proximity of war in Missouri led J. H. Lane, who was posing as Brigadier General of Volunteers, in command of Kansas troops, to "fortify" Fort Lincoln, on the Osage River. The work done there, in a military or common sense view, was simply idiotic. He went down on the very lowest bottom land of the river, where he threw up an earth-work about the size of a calf-pen and then blazoned it forth as a great military fortification.

In the latter part of August a considerable force was being concentrated at Fort Scott. Old Jim Montgomery had of course, by this time, gotten a regiment together, and five companies of the Third Kansas under him arrived on the 20th of August. Other Kansas troops arrived from time to time until the aggregate force was about two thousand men. Fort Scott was now headquarters for General Lane's brigade.

The rebel Generals, Price and Raines, were operating in Western Missouri with several thousand men, and contemplated an attack on Southeastern Kansas. On the 1st of September General Raines with his division approached within twelve miles of Fort Scott, on the southeast, and a scouting party came within two miles of town and captured a corral full of mules, and drove in Lane's pickets. A force of 500 cavalry with one 12 pound howitzer, was sent out the next day to reconnoitre. They ran into the rebel pickets and drove them across Drywood creek, where they were reinforced, and quite a rattling good skirmish was fought, until the ammunition of the Union forces gave out, when they fell back in good order on Fort Scott. The official reports give the Union loss in this action as five killed and twelve wounded. The rebel loss was about the same.

In the meantime the infantry force occupied the heights east and southeast of town. These troops were reinforced by an impromptu company, organized that morning, of such men as McDonald, Drake and the other citizens who were not already in line on the hill. This company was sworn into the service, drew arms and ammunition, and marched to the front in two rows like regulars. They still belong to the army. They were never mustered out. Some of them have their arms yet. Drake says his old musket is down in the cellar now, with the same load in it he put in on that day. Some of these days a little Lieutenant may come along and order them out on advance picket with three days' cooked rations, or he may order them to the Soldier's Home. They never drew pay. They are presumably entitled to back pay and bounty up to date. They are certainly all entitled to pensions by reason of rheumatism, superinduced by exposure while in line of duty. But they did their full duty that day, and if there had been a fight would have held on as long as anybody.

The entire force waited on the crest of the hill until night for the expected attack of General Raines. About dark a raging thunder storm—which follows after all great battles—came up, and the boys, concluding that it would affect the rebels just as it did them, returned to town and sought shelter in camp.

That night General Lane ordered the entire force to fall back on Fort Lincoln, twelve miles north, on the Osage, leaving Fort Scott to the mercy of anybody that might come along. A scouting party of fifty men could have gutted and burned the town without opposition. Lane displayed here his usual cowardice when confronted by real danger. It is said that he would have burned the town himself—had actually ordered the torch applied—but he was prevailed on by the citizens to wait at least until the rebel force had crossed the State line. Of course, there was great commotion in town. The non-combatants, women and children—excepting Mrs. Wm. Smith, Mrs. H. T. Wilson, Mrs. John S. Miller and one or two others, who decided to wait awhile,—were loaded into wagons and driven out west toward Marmaton. The torch was ready to be applied to every building in town on the first appearance of the rebel troops on the summit of the eastern hills. But they did not appear. General Raines was at that moment making a forced march on Lexington, Missouri, by an order that day received from General Price, and Fort Scott thus escaped utter annihilation.

THE SIXTH KANSAS.

The Sixth Kansas Cavalry was organized at Fort

Scott on the 9th of September, 1861. A large part of this regiment was Bourbon County men. W. R. Judson was Colonel. The first Lieutenant-Colonel was Lewis R. Jewell, who was killed at the battle of Cane Hill, Ark., November 28, 1862. W. T. Campbell was then promoted to Lieutenant-Colonel, and served through the war. Wyllys C. Ransom was Major. C. O. Judson was Adjutant until March, 1862. Isaac Stadden was then Adjutant until August, 1862. The Quartermasters were successively Geo. J. Clark, S. B. Gordon, Charles W. Jewell and Levi Bronson. Dr. John S. Redfield was surgeon until February 21, 1865, when he was mustered out and returned home. Capt. John Rogers, Captain of Company K, was killed by bushwhackers near the south line of this county on the 2nd of June, 1864. John G. Harris, lieutenant of Company K, was badly wounded at Cane Hill, Ark., by a ball passing clear through his neck. He recovered, and after the war was Sheriff of Bourbon County. The other line officers of the Sixth Kansas who lived in this county have been mentioned.

Jewell County in this State was named in honor of Colonel Lewis R. Jewell, when that County was organized in 1867, at the instance of Samuel A. Manlove, who was that year a member of the Legislature from Fort Scott.

Fort Scott was again established as a military post and a depot of supplies. From two thousand to ten thousand troops were making transitory stops here, arriving and departing and shifting about as the necessities of the case seemed to require. Long wagon trains of Government supplies,— hardtack, bacon, beans, rice, coffee and sugar, of the Commissary department, and blue uniforms, boots and shoes, blankets, etc., of the Quartermaster department were constantly coming and going, and the grand chorus of a thousand voices from the mule corral was the first thing heard in the morning and the last at night.

SOME MORE POLITICS.

In October, 1861, the Republican State Committee was petitioned by a large number of voters to nominate a State ticket, and a special and emphatic request was made in the petition that a patriotic and energetic man be named for Governor on a war platform. They claimed that Governor Charles Robinson was impotent and inefficient, and that by the terms of the State Constitution his term of office expired January 1, 1862, notwithstanding the enactment of the Legislature extending the term. The committee in response to these petitioners nominated a full State ticket with George A. Crawford, of Bourbon County, for Governor. There was no other ticket in the field for State officers. The location of the State Capital was to be voted on, and members of the Legislature were to be elected. The election was held on the 5th of November. Mr. Crawford and his ticket received more than one-half as many votes as the total vote polled on the State Capital question, but the State Board of Canvassers refused to canvass the vote. Mr. Crawford took the case to the Supreme Court, and it is the first case reported in the First Kansas reports. It is held by the Court that the act of the Legislature of May 22, 1861, provided for the election of Governor at the general election of 1862, and that the election of the Crawford ticket was null and void.

Topeka received the majority of the vote cast for State Capital.

Eli G. Jewell and Geo. A. Reynolds were elected to the Legislature from Bourbon County.

On the 2nd of December, 1861, General J. W. Denver was ordered to Fort Leavenworth, and placed in command of the Kansas troops.

CHAPTER XXV.

VARIOUS THINGS.

IN the Spring of 1862, a considerable force was concentrated at Fort Scott, consisting of the 1st and 6th Kansas, the 9th, 12th and 13th Wisconsin, the 2nd Ohio Cavalry and Captain Rabb's 2nd Indiana Battery. The 5th Kansas Cavalry, which had been camped at Barnesville all winter was placed under command of Col. Powell Clayton. In the early spring this regiment was marched through Fort Scott to Drywood. It remained there a few days, when Clayton got permission to take the regiment out of this department, and he hustled it off down on the lower Mississippi. Sam Walker, who has been mentioned several times during the border troubles was Major of this regiment. James Montgomery was Colonel of the 3d Kansas, and afterwards he was transferred to the command of a colored regiment in South Carolina, where he probably renewed his acquaintance with Buford and the Hamiltons, or at least with their kinfolks.

Speaking of the Hamiltons, nothing reliable is known of that particular group, after the war began. They all probably went into the rebel army. It is said that in the fall of 1861, Captain Bain, with a portion of the

6th Kansas, captured several persons over in Missouri, and on his way up he camped one night about two miles south of Arcadia. The next morning, after they had broken camp and started on the march, Bain took a detail of men, and, selecting out seven of the prisoners, took them off to one side of the road and killed them. Bain gave it out that they were with the Hamilton gang at the Marais des Cygnes murder. That was possibly true, but it was more probable that they were Bain's personal enemies

The Kansas troops had now been in the service several months, and they began to think they were old veterans. Most of them had quit writing letters to their folks more than twice a week, and they had all learned the best manner of cooking beans, and preparing hard-tack so that it would seem like something else. Their ideas of war were somewhat changed before they got through with it.

On the 10th of May, 1862, a small newspaper called the Fort Scott *Bulletin* was established.

In the spring of 1862 the people of Fort Scott let the city election go by default, and it was not until in August that they discovered they had missed a chance to vote. Then the council ordered an election to be held on the 25th. J. S. Miller was elected Mayor, H. T. Wilson, P. P. Elder, William Smith and C. F. Drake, Councilmen; J. E. Dillon, clerk: J. F. White, Marshal; C. W. Goodlander, Treasurer; A. R. Allison, Assessor, and J. G. Stuart, Street Commissioner.

On the 1st of June Lieutenant Colonel Lewis R.

Jewell was placed in command of the Post of Fort Scott.

About July, 1862, Rube Forbes, whom we have already had occasion to mention, and a man named Troy Dye robbed the store of E. S. Scott, at Xenia. This caused a great commotion among the settlers of that neighborhood, and they raised a posse, headed by Captain Vansycle, late of Co. "I," Sixth Kansas, and Lieutenant Ford of the same company. They got after the thieves in close chase. Dye got away but they run Forbes into a very dense brush patch about four miles south of Mapleton, where he was surrounded. The brush was so thick they could not see Rube but they charged in as far as they could and fired. Rube instantly returned the fire and Captain Vansycle fell dead. He fired again and Lieutenant Ford fell badly wounded. The lieutenant was at once taken up by Charles Love, J. R. Anderson and others, and carried on a coat to a house about half a mile distant, and was soon afterward taken to his home near Uniontown where he died. At the third fire by Rube, E. C. Buck was badly wounded in the neck, and came near dying. About that time a company of soldiers arrived, who fired a volley into the brush where Rube was and his dead body was dragged out.

On the 15th of July, 1862, the first number of the Bourbon County *Monitor* was issued at Marmaton by David B. Emmert.

The Second Kansas Battery was raised in Bourbon County by C. W. Blair, early in the summer. The officers were C. W. Blair, Captain; E. A. Smith,

D. C. Knowles, A. G. Clark, and A. Wilson, Lieutenants. This was known through the war as "Blair's Battery."

FALL ELECTIONS.

The general election in the State was held on the 4th of November, 1862. Thomas Carney, Republican, of Leavenworth, was elected Governor. He received exactly 10,000 votes. The opposition candidate was W. R. Wagstaff, of Paola. His vote was 5,463.

The vote in Bourbon County for Governor was 413 to 86. This county was the Fourteenth Senatorial District. Isaac Ford was elected Senator by 431 votes, against 33 votes for E. Williams. There were four Representative Districts in this county, the 50th, 51st, 52nd and 53rd. In the 50th D. B. Jackman received 41 votes, L. D. Clevenger, 26. In the 51st J. Hawkins, 62; W. T. Jones, 37. In the 52nd, D. R. Cobb received the entire vote, 97. In the 53rd, C. F. Drake received the entire vote, 205.

City Hall and Court House, 1865.

CHAPTER XXVI.

COUNTY SEAT RETURNED TO FORT SCOTT.

AT THIS session of the Legislature C. F. Drake introduced and had passed a general county seat law, providing for elections for county seats on petition to the County Court, etc. On the passage of that law the City Council of the City of Fort Scott, of which Mr. Drake was also a member, proposed to the County Court that the city would build a City Hall and in the event that the people, at the proposed election, voted to re-locate the county seat at Fort Scott the use of the City Hall would be given to the county for county purposes. The proposition was accepted by the Board of County Commissioners, and a special election for county seat was held on the 11th day of May, 1863. The result of the election was as follows: Fort Scott received 700 votes; Centerville, on Mill Creek, 279 votes; Mapleton, 14 votes; Fort Lincoln, 1 vote, and at a meeting of the Board of County Commissioners on the 16th of May 1863, the last one held at Marmaton, Fort Scott was by proclamation declared the county seat. At this meeting there were present T. W. Tallman, Isaac Ford and E. A. Toles, Commissioners and David R. Cobb, County Clerk.

The city council then took steps for the erection of the City Hall. The location decided on was the South-east corner of Locust and Jones streets, now Second Street and National Avenue. The building was to be of stone, two stories high. The contract was let to Goodlander & Allison for the sum of $3,900. It was completed that fall, except the railing around the spiral stairway, which was never finished. Goodlander made one for it but it didn't fit, and he threw it under the work bench, then he convinced the council that railings were out of style, anyhow.

At a meeting of the City Council held on December 14, 1863, it was on motion, ordered "That the City Marshal notify the county officers that the City Hall was in readiness, and request them to occupy the same."

The county officers then moved in. The County Clerk, Treasurer and Register of Deeds occupied the lower story. The District Court was held in the upper story. And that was the Bourbon County court house for nearly thirty years. When court was not in session the upper story was subject to be used for miscellaneous purposes. Religious services were held there nearly every Sunday by some Denomination which had, as yet, no home of their own. Political meetings and conventions caucused and pulled wires, and long-haired itinerant cranks would occasionally loosen the plastering in expounding their wonderful theories. During the 60's amateur dramatic clubs often "played" under the management of John R. Morley, Geo. Clark and Ken Williams, in a repertoire from "Black-eyed Susan" to "Hamlet." A "Masquerade Ball" was given at least once a year. The "Masques" were varied, most life-like, and always thoroughly original.

But few incidents of local interest transpired during the year 1863. There was not much done in the way of improvement either in the town or county. The erection of the woollen factory by Geo. A. Crawford was the most important. Fort Scott being a military post, a telegraph line was constructed from Fort Leavenworth, and the people had means of communication with the outside world, without having to depend on the often delayed trips of the old "jerky" stage, which the boys said was a "tri-weekly,—it went out one week and tried to get back the next." Sometimes it didn't do it. The stage fare between Kansas City and Fort Scott was "ten dollars and carry a rail." Sometimes, when the roads were real good, a man passenger would not have to walk and carry a rail more than a third of the time. When they were very bad he walked all the way, carried his rail, and paid his ten dollars just the same. So. But then he had the privilege of being whirled into town and landed at the Wilder House with a grand flourish. That was worth something.

A good portion of the men of Bourbon County, in common with those of the balance of the State, were in the army. The total number of Kansas troops in the field by the middle of this year was 9,600. A large number went in after that date. Nearly every man living in Kansas during the war was in the service in some shape. If not in the volunteer service he was in the home guards or State militia.

On the 4th of July, 1863, E. A. Smith was promoted to Captain of the 2nd Kansas, or Blair's Battery, and Blair was assigned to the 14th Regiment of Kansas Volunteers as Colonel. He was soon after promoted to Brigadier General, and ordered to Fort Scott as commandant of the post. He remained in command of this post until April 28th, 1865, when he was succeeded by Gen. U. B. Pearsall, who remained in command until the close of the war.

ELECTIONS.

The general election in the State was held on the 3rd of November. District Attorneys, Legislators, and a part of the county officers were to be chosen. Samuel A. Riggs was elected District Attorney for the Fourth Judicial District, consisting of the counties of Allen, Anderson, Bourbon, Douglas, Franklin, Johnson, Linn and Miami. The Representatives for Bourbon County were Wm. Stone, R. P. Stevens, D. R. Cobb and J. G. Miller. County Treasurer, James Aitkin; Sheriff, H. G. Moore; Probate Judge, Wm. Rose; Register of Deeds, E. B. Norcross. The new County Board was organized on the next January: T. W. Tallman, E. A. Toles and J. F. Holt, Commissioners, and J. S. Emmert, County Clerk.

FORT BLAIR, Built in the Street at the Corner of Scott Avenue and First Street in the Spring of 1864.

CHAPTER XXVII.

FORTIFICATIONS.

IN the early part of 1864 several extensive fortifications were commenced, and finished that spring. These were quite heavy, well constructed earthworks. "Fort Henning" was located on Second street, between National Avenue and Judson street. "Fort Blair" was on First street between Main street and Scott Avenue, and contained the block house now standing across from the post office. "Fort Insley" was on the extreme point northeast of the Plaza. There were some barracks and fortifications commenced on the hill southeast of town, and some rifle pits on what we now call Tower Hill. The old Government Hospital building was used for a hospital, and the old guard house was again utilized for the original purpose.

Dr. Van Duyn was the surgeon in charge of hospitals at this post during 1864.

POLITICAL FEELING.

There was but little partisan political feeling in this County at that time. Public sentiment may have found vent, to some extent, in the action of the City Council at a meeting held January 2, at which Councilmen Dimon, White and Drake caused the following order to be spread upon the minutes:

"*Ordered:* That the Street Commissioner cause a sidewalk to be built from the corner of Wall Street, etc., and *provided*, that said walks be of two planks one foot wide, 12 inches apart, 2½ inches thick, slightly elevated, and pinned to terra firma like h—l."

The old party organizations were kept up, but the sentiments of all were simply for the Union and for the suppression of the rebellion.

At a large Democratic convention held May 23rd, 1864, in the City Hall, for the purpose of electing a delegate to the State Democratic Convention to be held at Topeka, the following resolution, among others, was passed:

"*Resolved*, That we will vote for no man for President or Vice-President who is not pledged to devote all his powers to the suppression of the rebellion, and maintain and defend the Constitution of the Union from all aggression from secession traitors of the South and conspirators of the North."

The meeting was presided over by Robert Blackett. O. Dieffenbaugh was secretary. Charles Bull was chosen delegate to the State Convention.

John E. Himoe, of Mapleton, brother of Dr. S. O. Himoe, while on a trip up the Missouri river, about April 1, 1864, was taken down with the smallpox. He was landed at Boonville with a nurse. While there he became delirious and one night, escaping from the house in that condition, he tried to break in through the window of a neighboring house, and the man inside

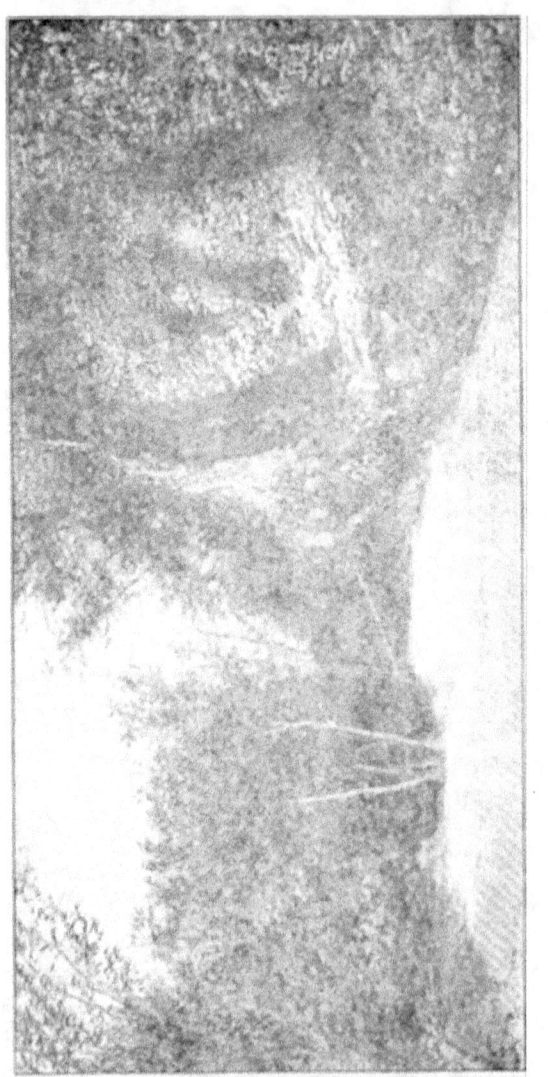

Scene on Drywood, near South Line of the County.

naturally took him for a burglar and shot him dead. Mr. Himoe was at that time County Surveyor of this county.

RAIDS ON DRYWOOD.

About the 20th of May, 1864, Henry Taylor, a noted guerrilla of Vernon County, Mo., made a raid in the Drywood valley. He had a large company with him, some say as many as eighty men. He entered Bourbon County on the south, and first went to the house of William Custard, about ten o'clock at night. Custard had been in bed, but by some means he got warning of their approach, and he and his brother, Rufus, made their escape, just in the nick of time. Taylor run into the house and, in the search, he felt in the warm bed, which Custard had just left.

Taylor then robbed several families and committed other depredations. Finally, on his return out of the county he went to the house of Louis L. Ury, at the place where Garland is now, and surrounded it. There were in the house, Mr. Ury and his wife, his son Joe Ury, and the young children, Newt and the two girls, now Mrs. Homer Pond and Mrs. John Withers, and a Mr. T. Cartmell. Taylor had with him Mike Kelley, John Gwynn and several other prisoners that he had picked up, and intended to get Mr. Ury and his son Joe. After capturing the men folks he moved Newt and the two girls out into the corner of the yard preparatory to burning the house. Just then George Pond, James Pitts and Fred Carpenter, a scouting party from the 3d Wisconsin Cavalry, run onto them and commenced firing, and Joe Ury, as soon as he heard the guns, picked up a stick of wood and knocked Taylor down. When Taylor got up, he called out "shoot the prisoners," and made for his horse. Some of the others of the gang fired at the prisoners, two balls striking Mr. Louis Ury, who was standing in his door. Then the entire party lit out for Missouri, leaving all the prisoners. Mr. Ury's wounds were found to be very serious. His leg had to be amputated and he lingered until the 2nd of July, when he died.

The summer before this occurred, this same Taylor captured a man by the name of Tom Whitesides from the house of Mrs. Beal's, east of Fort Scott, and took him to near the "Line House" and killed him, firing twelve shots into him. After the war Taylor was elected sheriff of Vernon county.

About June 1, 1864, a dozen or more bushwhackers made a raid into the county, up on the head of Pawnee Creek, and captured Rev. Mr. Harryman, Mr. Potter, and two or three colored people, and robbed and burned Mr. Harryman's house. The robbers took alarm at the approach of some parties and hastily left without their prisoners.

RAILROADS—POLITICS.

On the 1st day of June, 1864, a railroad convention in the interest of the Border Tier railway was held at Paola. The delegates from Bourbon County were Geo. A. Crawford, Geo. Dimon, H. T. Wilson, Isaac Stadden, Dr. Freeman and A. Danford. D. P. Lowe and J. D. Snoddy were among those from Linn County.

This was the first concerted effort in the direction of building railroads in this section of the State. Speeches were made and various committees appointed. One committee was appointed to memorialize Congress to grant lands to a border road, setting forth in their memorial the vast importance of such a road in a military point of view. The people had sat down to an indefinite siege of war. The end seemed far off in the dim future, and they had come to accept it as almost the natural condition.

President Lincoln was nominated for re-election. An immense ratification meeting was held on the 20th day of June, 1864, at Fort Scott. T. T. Insley was President, and J. R. Morley, J. F. White, W. A. Shannon, B. P. McDonald, S. A. Manlove, and Wm. Margrave were Vice-Presidents.

At the Democratic Convention of Topeka, J. Thomas Bridgens of Fort Scott, was appointed one of the candidates for Presidential Elector.

A Republican State Convention met at Topeka on the 8th of September, 1864. On the first ballot for candidate for Governor, George A. Crawford was in the lead, but the opposition concentrated on Samuel J. Crawford, and on the sixth ballot the vote stood: Samuel J. Crawford, 51; Geo. A. Crawford, 31; and Samuel J. Crawford was declared the nominee.

THE PRICE RAID.

In October, 1864, what is called the Price Raid took place. General Price passed up from Arkansas through

Central Missouri, in the direction of Lexington, on the Missouri river. He recruited his army as he advanced until he had about 20,000 effective men. General S. R. Curtis was at Leavenworth, in command of the Department of Kansas. General Curtis's command consisted of part of the 14th and all of the 15th and 16th Kansas, a battalion of the 3rd Wisconsin, a section of the 2d Kansas Battery, a Colorado battery, and the 9th Wisconsin Battery, a total of about 4,500 men. On the 8th of October he proclaimed martial law, and ordered all the U. S. troops into the field to resist Price. Governor Carney called out the State Militia, and ordered them to the Border under General Deitzler, Major General of State Militia. At Fort Scott there were assembled from various points 1,050 men. The most of these were formed into the 24th Regiment of State Militia, with the following field and staff officers: Colonel, Isaac Stadden; Lieutenant Colonel, John Van Fossen; Major, Joseph Ury; Adjutant, A. Danford; Quartermaster, J. Thomas Bridgens; Surgeons, B. F. Hepler and S. O. Himoe.

The companies in the 24th Regiment were officered as follows: Company A, John F. White and C. B. Hayward; Company B, W. C. Dennison and R. D. Lender; Company C, J. B. Skeen, Thomas Barnes and C. B. Maurice; Company D, J. C. Hinkley and Robt. Stalker; Company E, H. T. Coffman, R. Adams and W. P. Gray; Company F, J. C. Ury, J. B. Cabiness and S. Streeter.

Lieutenant Colonel George P. Eaves, of Uniontown, had a battalion of mounted men, which he raised in the various townships of the county, consisting of seven

companies, which had the following named officers:
Company A, D. D. Roberts, I. Burton and C. W. Campbell; Company B, Dyer Smith, D. R. Radden and B. R. Wood; Company C, John J. Stewart, John Blair and E. M. Marshall; Company D, S. B. Mahurin, John Hamilton and J. C. Andrick; Company E, B. F. Gumm, Nathan Baker and William Goff; Company F, Isaac Morris, R. S. Stevens and A. S. Potter; Company G, W. A. Shannon, N. J. Roscoe and D. McComas.

These troops were soon reinforced by militia from Allen and Coffey counties, under Colonel Twiss and Major Goss.

With Colonel Eaves' force and all the mounted troops he could pick up, General Blair left for the field to join Blunt's division, then near Westport, Missouri.

Generals Pleasanton and Sanborn, with about 4,000 men had left Jefferson City, to join the general pursuit.

On the 20th, 21st and 22d, engagements took place respectively at Lexington, Little Blue and Big Blue. The Union troops were victorious. Price was rapidly retreating down the Missouri border, fighting almost continuously. He had 15,000 veteran troops, plenty of field artillery, and such lieutenants as Shelby, Marmaduke, Cabell, Slemmon, Fagan and Graham. Price's army first entered Kansas in Linn county, and a part of it camped, on the 24th of October, just north of the Trading Post, on the exact spot at the base of the big mound near old Jackey Williams' farm, where, on that beautiful May day in 1858, the forerunners of this army of invasion had enacted the prologue of the bloody and disastrous scene which was to follow on the next day.

The old gray haired General could still see on that hallowed ground

>"The blush as of roses
>Where rose never grew;
>Great drops on the bunch grass
>But not of the dew."

And in his troubled sleep that night, when the lights burned blue, at the dead of midnight, there may have come to him the visions of those murdered men, as

>"With no vain plea for mercy,
>No stout knee was crooked;
>In the mouths of the rifles
>Right manly they looked.
>How paled the May sunshine,
>Green Marais du Cygne,
>When the death-smoke blew over
>Thy lonely ravine!"

On the 25th of October, after a sharp skirmish, the rebel forces retreated to the south side of the Marais des Cygnes, and the entire army was brought to bay, and was formed in line of battle in Mine Creek Valley, near where now stands the City of Pleasanton. It was a grand field for a battle. The open prairie was four or five miles in extent, with only gentle undulations, and the entire force, as well as all the maneuvers of either army, could be plainly seen. The troops under General Blair, Colonel Moonlight and Colonel Crawford were in position nearly on the left flank of the enemy, with Generals Pleasanton, Sanborn, McNiel and Benteen on the center and right. The engagement was general, and for some hours well and hotly contested.

Finally, a brilliant movement was made by Colonels Philips and Benteen, and a brigade under General Cabell of nearly 1000 men was captured, together with nine pieces of artillery. Generals Marmaduke, Cabell, Slemmer and Graham were also taken prisoners. The enemy now rapidly retreated, their deflection into Missouri, to the southeast, being forced in a great measure by the field maneuvers of General Blair and Colonel Crawford.

Another stand was made by the enemy on the Little Osage in Bourbon County, but McNiel and Pleasanton, who were in advance, soon routed them out; and still another on Shiloh Creek in this county, where we captured two pieces of artillery.

RAIDS BY GUERILLAS.

On the 20th of October, just before the battle of Mine Creek occurred, a squad of about twenty-five men, belonging to the command of the old guerilla, Jo Shelby, struck the Osage river about the State line, and went up on the north side. When they got up to Fort Lincoln, they halted in front of the store in that place, owned by Knowles & Green. Andrew Stevens and W. H. Green were near the store door. The bushwhackers at once opened fire on the two men, and Stevens was instantly killed. Green escaped by slipping down under the river bank and making for the brush. Then they plundered the store and burned the building, and the residences of Mr. Knowles, Mr. Green and Mr. Hopkins, after robbing Mrs. Hopkins.

They then crossed the river, and robbed all the families living as far west as Primm's and Armstrong's, and burned the dwellings, hay stacks, and barns belonging to Dick Stafford. Turning back down the Osage, and dividing up into squads, they killed Mr. Woodall and Mr. Miller.

MARMATON MASSACRE.

Another raid by guerrillas was made into Bourbon County on the 22nd of October, 1864. On Saturday night of that date, about midnight a company of from forty to sixty men, under command of Allen Matthews and Major Courcey, came up from a southern direction to the neighborhood of Marmaton. Before they reached town some of the neighboring farmers had discovered them and came in ahead and gave the alarm. That night there were about thirty Home Guards quartered in the church, under command of Captain Harding, First Lieutenant Ramsey, and Second Lieutenant J. G. Roush. By order of Captain Harding these men were scattered out in squads of eight or ten to picket the several roads leading into town. In the meantime, the guerrillas, presuming such would be the case, left the main road and charged across lots into town, which they thus found without any defense at all. They then commenced capturing every man they could get hold of, and firing on any they saw trying to run away. They first picked up Colonel Horatio Knowles, Daniel M. Brown, Dr. L. M. Chadwick, Joseph Stout, Abner McGonigle and Warren Hawkins. These men they murdered in the most cold-blooded manner, as fast as they came to them, in some instances taking hold of their victim with one hand and putting a bullet through his head from a revolver in the other. In other cases they would repeatedly shoot into their prisoners while they were down and begging for mercy.

Nelson Ramsey, Wm. Holt, brother of Judge Holt, Rev. Mr. Prigmore, and others, were on the street, and were repeatedly fired at, but they slipped away somehow and hid in the deep ravines near by.

The stores in town were those of Aitkin & Knowles, and Cobb & Jones. These they robbed and then burned. The residence of Mrs. Schoen, widow of Lieutenant Schoen, of Company E, 10th Kansas, the Methodist church, and other buildings were burned.

As soon as possible after the attack, Lieutenant Roush started for Fort Scott to give the alarm and get help in the pursuit of the ruffians. Some of them discovered him and gave him close chase as far as the Catholic Cemetery, when they probably concluded they were near the Fort Scott picket line, and turned back. Lieutenant Roush reported the affair to Colonel Stadden, who ordered out a force in pursuit, but the bushwhackers had too much the start, and being well mounted they got away. In passing out of the county, near Cato, they killed another man, a Mr. Simons, whom Matthews had a special grudge against. They then continued their flight into the Cherokee Nation.

Reliable information is furnished that this Matthews with about twenty of his men, left soon after for the Rocky Mountains, going in a north-westerly direction into the country of the Osage Indians. At a crossing of the Verdigris river, near where Independence now is, and just after they had crossed, they were met by a large body of Osages who informed them that the Osage people had orders to arrest any and all persons attempting to pass through their country and take them to Fort Scott. Matthews told them they were friends of the tribe, but that they would never submit to be taken alive, especially as prisoners to Fort Scott. A battle then opened, and Matthews and every one of his men were killed. This is the statement as made by Little Bear, who was then Chief of the Osages.

The murders recounted in these raids were the most atrocious and cold-blooded of any that had ever occurred in Bourbon County. The men killed were all good, quiet, peaceable citizens, not identified in any way as partisans, or even active in politics, excepting Horatio Knowles, who had been in the Legislature several years, as has been noted. It was probably not known at the time to what particular rebel command these murderers belonged who raided the Osage valley. The statement is made here that they belonged to the command of the rebel General Jo Shelby, although he was not present in person. The proof of it is given in the following extracts from page 447 of a book published in 1867 by authority of Shelby, called "Shelby and His Men; or War in the West." The author says, in speaking of these raids into Kansas:

"No prisoners were taken, and why should there be? * * Shelby was leaving Kansas and taking terrible adieus. * * Hay stacks, houses, barns, produce, crops, and farming implements were consumed before the march of his squadrons, and what the flames spared the bullet finished. Shelby was soothing the wounds of Missouri by stabbing the breast of Kansas. For the victims of Lane and Jennison he demanded life for life and blood for blood. The interest had been compounded, but he gathered it to the utmost farthing. Fort Scott lay before him like a picture, mellowed by haze and distance, and the orders for its destruction had gone forth."

And the orders for its destruction would have been fully carried out had it not been for the prompt organization and assembly of the militia.

Price had also determined on the total destruction of the City of Fort Scott. Marmaduke and other rebel officers, while prisoners of war here, repeatedly stated that Price had given orders for the annihilation of Fort Scott as soon as they could get to it.

SUSPENSE.

On the day of the battle of Mine Creek, and for some days previous, the people of Fort Scott and the troops here were naturally in a state of great suspense. They knew, indefinitely, that there had been fighting up north, and that Price was retreating down the border. They had good reason to fear the worst. They had no disposition to cry wolf when there was no wolf, and they fully realized their danger if the rebel army should get at them, and they were nerved up to defend themselves to the best of their ability. They probably did not know at that time of the especial determination and order to destroy the town, but in a general way they

knew Price and his men and his methods, and they had
every reason to believe that he would attack and destroy
Fort Scott, which was then rich in supplies and plunder.

A part of the defensive force was posted on the hills
north of town. Entrenchments were thrown up at the
river fords, and preparations made for moving the women
and children.

About 3 o'clock on the morning of the 25th the
cannon boomed forth the alarm. A scout had just
arrived with the news that the enemy was at the
Trading Post, and it was presumed that their march on
Fort Scott would be unchecked. Every man was at
his post, and all exhibited the coolness of veteran
troops. The morning was rainy, but it cleared up later
in the forenoon, Up to 3 o'clock that afternoon no
definite news was had of the operations of the two
armies. They could hear the boom of the cannon, but
they did not know the result of the day. All kinds
of rumors were flying. Late in the day large bodies
of troops were seen marching on the city. But it was
soon ascertained that they were Union troops under
Colonel Moonlight. They then learned of the victory
at Mine Creek, and that General Blair's command and
other forces of the Union army would soon be here.
The revulsion of feeling cannot be described. The
tense, rigid feeling of suspense and anxiety which had
so long held the courageous militia to their work, gave
way to exultation and joy.

That night Generals Curtis, Pleasanton, Blunt and
Sanborn and their forces came in, bringing the captured
rebel Generals and other prisoners, and the captured

cannon. The next morning they again took up the march in pursuit of Price, except General Pleasanton and his command, who, after remaining a few days, left for St. Louis with the prisoners and captured artillery.

On the 28th, Colonel Stadden of the 24th regiment, issued the following order:

Gen. Order No. 5.

The Colonel commanding takes pleasure at this time in thanking the brave men under his command for the heroism and fortitude displayed during the late crisis. Although not actively engaged in the field, the cheerfulness displayed is certainly worthy of a veteran corps.

* * * * Again he assures you that no one will have occasion to blush for being a member of the "First Bourbon."   I. STADDEN,
A. DANFORD, Adjutant.   Colonel Commanding.

PUBLIC MEETING.

On the next Saturday evening a large public meeting was held in Fort Scott. S. A. Manlove was chosen President, and J. R. Morley, George Dimon, G. A. Reynolds, N. Z. Strong and William Margrave, Vice-Presidents. General Blair, who had returned to his post as Commandant, was called on to speak. The General said he was not there to make a political speech, as he had nothing to do with politics since the war began, and would not have until it closed. He said he desired, however, to do justice to the brave men who had left their homes and kept in the front until Kansas was out of danger. He closed with a detailed description of the battle of Mine Creek, and the military operations along the Border.

As has been stated, General Curtis continued the chase after the rebels, pursuing them to their final destruction as an army.

This was the last time Bourbon County was threatened by the invasion of an armed enemy, and the people soon settled down to some degree of peace and quiet.

The general election was held on the 8th day of November. Samuel J. Crawford was elected Governor and Sidney Clarke, Congressman; A. Danford was elected State Senator from Bourbon County. The Representatives were: Fiftieth District, L. D. Clevenger; Fifty-first, D. L. Campbell; Fifty-second, N. Griswold; Fifty-third, N. Z. Strong. D. M. Valentine was elected Judge of the Fourth Judicial District. D. B. Emmert, District Clerk; Wm. Margrave, Probate Judge, and Nelson Griswold, Superintendent of Schools.

Bourbon County cast 960 votes for Lincoln electors and 126 for the McClellan electors.

The year 1864 had been a season of more than usual disquietude and apprehension, in this county. Besides the operations of the regular Confederate armies, there were many roving bands of guerillas, bushwhackers and marauders swarming along the Missouri border, who took every opportunity to slip into Kansas and commit murder, robbery, theft and any depredation that took their fancy or that occasion permitted.

The bordering section of Missouri was practically without law, civil or military, and these men held full sway in their reign of terror. This state of affairs continued until Price's horde was swept down the Border, and the last remnant of rebellion disappeared.

CHAPTER XXVIII.

LINCOLN.

THE year 1865, while it was laden with events of vast import to the Nation, bore to us but few marked incidents of a local nature. President Lincoln was re-inaugurated on the 4th of March, and was assassinated on the 14th of April. He had, however, lived to see the surrender of Appomattox, and to smilingly approve of Grant's direction to the paroled army of North Virginia: "Take your horses and mules home, you will need them on the farm." He had lived to see the rebellion crushed, and to realize that government by the people should not perish from the earth. Nor will his name. He had reached the apex of human greatness. The Infinite fittingly ordained there should be no descent.

CITY ELECTION.

In the spring of 1865 the regular election was held in Fort Scott for city officers. Isaac Stadden was elected Mayor. The Councilmen were A. R. Allison, S. A. Manlove, Charles Rubicam and J. R. Morley. City Marshal, H. C. Jones; Treasurer, C. F. Drake; Recorder, Wm. Margrave; Assessor, J. W. Coutant;

Street Commissioner, C. W. Goodlander ; Attorney, A. Danford.

THE SCHOOLS.

In January, 1860, S. W. Greer, Superintendent of Schools, made a report of the condition of the schools in the Territory at that date. His figures for Bourbon County are as follows : Number of districts organized, seven. Number of children between the ages of 5 and 21, seventy-four.

The first school district in this county was organized in December, 1859. It was what was afterwards District No. 10. None were organized in 1860, and only 45 were organized until after the war, when in 1867 the organization of districts again commenced. At the close of 1865 there were 3,261 children of school age in the county. Many of these were children of refugees who had come in to Fort Scott from Missouri and Arkansas. Through the efforts of C. F. Drake, and a few others, school rooms were furnished and fitted up in the old hospital building and in the old City Hall.

The few school buildings in the county were poorly furnished. The appliances were meager. There was nothing like uniformity in books. The children brought the books which had been used by their parents fifteen or twenty years before, and represented nearly as many different States and kinds of books as there were children. The daily routine was something like this: The reading class would form in line; one scholar read a verse from an old reader commencing, "Rome was an ocean of flame;" the next would read one about

"Lo! the Poor Indian;" the next, not having anything but Webster's Spelling Book, read about one of the pictures in the back part, where the girl failed to be able to buy a new dress because the cow kicked over the pail of milk. And so on down the line, until the last one, a little fellow, read the best he could about the wonderful cat.

The facilities for acquiring an education in those times compares but feebly with our grand institutions of the present day. Our trained, competent and efficient professional teachers, with the paternal aid of the State, have wrought a wonderful change. Working through our Normal Colleges and High Schools, they have brought our common school system wellnigh to perfection. Not only that, they have caused the word "Teacher" to take its rightful place at the head of the list of the learned professions. And also, like Abou Ben-Adhem, "of those who love their fellow-men, their names lead all the rest." "May their tribe increase."

COST OF PROVISIONS.

In July, 1865, J. S. Emmert, County Clerk, left among the records of the County an itemized account of the expenses of housekeeping, from which the following extracts are made:

One-half bushel apples, $1.50; one dozen beets, 50 cents; four pounds of butter, $1.25; four dozen eggs, $1.30; four heads of cabbage, 50 cents; twelve pounds of sugar, $3.00; five pounds of coffee, $5.00; one-half gallon kerosene, $1.00; one bushel of potatoes, $2.00;

six bars soap, $1.00 ; two chickens, 80 cents ; one peck of onions, 75 cents; one-half pound tea $1.50; fifty pounds flour, $3.50.

MUSTER-OUT.

The Kansas troops had been or were being mustered out. Their old yellow parchments said they were "honorably discharged." "No objection to re-enlistment known to exist." But many of them knew there were objections known to exist—dressed in calico—and they were going to meet those objections, just as soon as possible. A farewell glance was given the faithful old camp kettles and mess pans, in which they had so often cooked coffee and beans and rice and desiccated potatoes, or the chickens and sweet potatoes, turkeys, and pigs, and geese, which somehow found their way into the company messes. They were going home. The orderly sergeant called the roll for the last time. He skipped many names on the original muster-in roll. Some had been discharged for wounds or other disability; many had left their bones in one or the other of a dozen States from Kansas to the Sea.

The record of Kansas in the war is grand. The State sent more soldiers to the war than it had voters in 1861. Its quota under the calls for troops was 12,931; it sent 20,151, without conscription. Nineteen regiments and three batteries participated in more than a hundred engagements, six of which were on Kansas soil. The battlefields from Wilson Creek to the Gulf are consecrated by their blood. Provost-Marshal-General Fry, in his final reports of the Union Army Roster, wrote this: "Kansas shows the highest battle mortality of the table. The same singular martial disposition which induced about one-half of the able-bodied men to enter the army without bounty may be supposed to have increased their exposure to the casualties of battle after they were in the service."

The regiments and batteries had all made an honorable record. In the many battles in which they were engaged, there were none of which they were not entitled by General Orders to emblazon the battle-name on the white stripes of "Old Glory."

BUSINESS AND IMPROVEMENT.

The people of our county were now turning their attention more than ever before to the pursuits of peace.

For ten years there had existed among our entire people a sense of insecurity and apprehension. It was an epoch of unrest,—a decade of bloody strife. No one on retiring to rest at night knew what might occur before another sun. An enemy was always in striking distance. They became accustomed to this state of affairs at times, when the recurrence of some bloody deed would again raise up the nightmare of border strife or civil war.

But all that was at an end. The war was over, and the receding tide had taken with it the flotsam and jetsam of border war.

Fort Scott was rapidly improving. The "Wilder House" and the stone "Miller Block," opposite, had been built sometime, and they were classed among the architectural wonders of the State.

The Wilder House was thus named in compliment to A. C. Wilder, who was Congressman from this State, and afterwards stationed for a time at Fort Scott in the Commissary Department, and who was, also, a great friend of the Dimon brothers, who built the house. A. C. Wilder was a brother of D. W. Wilder, who is not only well known in Fort Scott but throughout the West.

The "Miller Block" was built by Dr. J. G. Miller, who, as stated, was a Representative in 1865, and a prominent man until his death, some time afterwards.

The military telegraph had been run down the road from Leavenworth in 1863, and its last months of use here by the military, the office was conducted by J. D. McCleverty as chief operator. George A. Crawford had erected a year before a large flouring mill of four run of burrs, probably the largest mill then in the State. Early this year he commenced the erection of a large woollen factory, the largest and best appointed of any one in the West. By fall of this year there could be heard the whirr of a thousand spindles, and the intermittent thump and bang of many looms. The best grade of merchant yarns, blankets, and woollen cloths were manufactured. The wheat and wool of this and adjoining counties were worked up here which found a ready market. This mill and factory were totally destroyed by fire on the night of November 1, 1870. There was no insurance on this property and its loss to Mr. Crawford caused much financial embarrassment. It was also a severe blow to the city of Fort Scott. These mills were the pride of the town, then struggling for a

SECTION OF MARKET STREET, 1865.

place in the front rank of the manufacturing points in this State, and ambitious even then, to be rated as the principal city of Southern Kansas.

The establishment of a military post at Fort Scott during the war was, of course, of material advantage to it. While much of the business was of a transitory nature, a very considerable amount of it was of legitimate wholesale trade, and the retail trade with the surrounding country was very extensive.

Among the largest business houses at the close of 1865 may be noted the following: Dry Goods—Wilson, Gordon & Ray, A. McDonald & Bro., J. F. White, J. R. Morley & Co., Wm. Roach, Rosenfield & Co., Sanderson & Thomas, Shannon & Seavers, A. J. Lagore, and Jones & Cobb. Groceries—Linn & Stadden, G. R. Bodine, A. Cohen, Ernich & Lender, E. M. Insley, Van Fossen Bros., Parker & Tomlinson, and Pennington & Secrist. Hardware—C. F. Drake and Rubicam & Dilworth. Bankers—A. McDonald & Bro. Book Store—S. A. Manlove. Livery Stables—Benj. Files, P. Clough, H. Dimon, S. A. Olds, and Chas. Walker. Watch Maker—D. Prager. Tailors—R. Blackett and J. Winter. Harness Maker—Hartman & Co. Plasterer—A. Coston. Shoemaker—John Crow. Cabinet Makers—S. O. Goodlander and Wm. C. Weatherwax. Wagon Maker—John A. Bryant. Blacksmiths—W. H. Dory, Moses Boire and C. J. Neal. Drug Stores—D. S. Andrick & Co. and W. C. Dennison & Co. Barbers—Ed. Henderson and Joe Barker. Carpenter—C. W. Goodlander. Masons—John Higgins and Billy Shannehan. Physicians—B. F. Hepler, J. H. Couch, J. S.

Redfield, S. O. Himoe, L. M. Timmonds, J. C. Van Pelt, etc. Lawyers—Too many, as usual.

The rest of the fellows kept saloons.

The principal business part of the town was then on Market street—called Bigler street then—and North Main street. A. McDonald & Bro.'s store was in a long one-story frame house, fronting on Scott avenue, and running along Wall street to the alley. The "Banking House" was in the rear end of it, with an entrance on Wall street.

The other business houses, on Market and Main Streets, were all one and two story frame buildings, many of them but little better than board shanties. Most of the business houses on these streets were burned in the great fire of April 23, 1873.

A very good county fair was held at Fort Scott on October 12, 1865. G. A. Crawford, David Gardner, A. Goff, and N. C. Hood, were the officers.

The general election for 1865, was held on the 2nd of November. In Bourbon County D. B. Emmert was elected as State Senator to fill a vacancy. The Representatives elected were as follows: 50th District, W. H. Green; 51st, J. L. Wilson; 52nd, Nelson Griswold; 53rd, C. W. Blair. General Blair ran against W. A. Shannon, a very popular republican, and was elected by a vote of 264, as against 145 for Shannon.

The ruling prices of some of the staple provisions in the fall and winter of 1865, in the Fort Scott market were as follows: Wheat, $2.50 per bushel; flour, $10 per hundred; corn meal, $2.75 per bushel; oats, $2 per bushel; corn, $2.50 per bushel; sugar, 33 to 50c per pound; coffee, Rio, 66¼c per pound; coffee, Java, 75c per pound; teas, $2.50 to $3.50 per pound; rice, 30c per pound; molasses, $1.50 to $3 per gallon; butter, 50c per pound; cheese, 40c per pound; eggs, 60c per dozen; potatoes, $4 to $4.50 per bushel; turnips, $2 per bushel; green apples, $3.50 to $4 per bushel; dried apples, $5 per bushel.

In the summer of 1865 the Kansas & Neosho Valley Railroad Company was organized at Kansas City, Mo. The initial point of this road was to be at Kansas City. The Southern terminus and direction was undetermined. Official communication was opened with our County Board with a view to having Bourbon County take $150,000 in stock of the Company. After some correspondence the Board finally required that the name of Fort Scott be incorporated in the name of the Company and road, and suggested "Missouri River, Fort Scott & Gulf" as such name. The Company at once agreed to make the change, and at a meeting on November 18th, the Board ordered an election to be held on the 16th day of December, 1865, on the question of voting $150,000 in county bonds. The election resulted as follows: Osage Township voted 41 for, none against; Freedom 65 for, 4 against; Timberhill 49 for, 33 against; Franklin 4 for, 87 against; Marion 17 for, 67 against; Marmaton 36 for, 29 against; Scott 493 for, none against. Total, 705 for, and 220 against. And the first preliminary struggle for a railroad through Bourbon County was over. This road was completed to Fort Scott in the fall of 1869.

In November, 1865, County Assessor, Mr. E. Brown,

made his official returns, from which the following figures are taken:

Population — White males, 4,954; white females, 4,282; black males, 379; black females, 418. Total population of the county, 10,033. Fort Scott contained about 1,800 inhabitants, who were actual citizens. The total valuation, real and personal, (which the assessor returned together) of the entire county, was $1,442,687.00. During the fiscal year of 1865 there was harvested and manufactured the amounts and articles following: Wheat harvested, 28,676 bushels. Rye, 3,621; Corn, 206,297; Oats, 15,352. Irish potatoes, 5,591; sweet potatoes, 821. Butter, 14,498 lbs. Cheese, 11,907 pounds. Sorghum molasses, 7,606 gallons. Hay, 15,565 tons. Total number of acres of land fenced, 34,344.

Acres of land improved, 25,687. Number of horses, 2,702; number of mules, 301; number of milch cows, 3,630; number of oxen, 603; number of other cattle, 5,209; number of sheep, 6,345; number of swine, 2,638. Value of live stock, $476,295.

The population of the county had increased about 4,000 since the enumeration of 1860.

There was no census, even approximate, of the population of Fort Scott in 1865. There was a large "floating population" of refugees and indiscriminate and indescribable people, white and black, who had, practically, no home or residence anywhere, to the number of 1,000 or more. The actual number of bona fide citizens was probably less than 1,800. The tax roll of the city bears less than 400 names.

Opera House Corner and North Main Street, 1865.

THE CLOSE.

The close of the year 1865, is deemed the fitting period to close this volume of the History of Bourbon County. It is the closing point of an Era. Old "Time" here rested his scythe for a moment, and turned the sand in his glass.

A final tribute should be paid to our men and women, one and all, the living and the dead, who came to this county in early times to help found a State.

They sacrificed all the established comforts of their homes in the old States to found new homes in this semi-wilderness. They came with no misunderstanding as to the state of the country or the political and social conditions. They came with their eyes wide open, each well knowing that his life here, for many years, must be and would be a life of hardship, self-denial and danger. As a class, they were a superior people; superior in that stamina of character; superior in that native manhood and womanhood which goes to make up the "salt of the earth." Poor they were in purse, but rich in integrity of purpose.

At the old fireside, a young man, "the flower of the flock," the one widest between the eyes, stood out from the family circle and said : "Sis, pack my carpet-bag, I'm going to Kansas." "Sis" was probably to follow as soon as a certain young man had a cabin and ten acres of sod corn.

And so they came. Sometimes one, alone, sometimes the entire family.

Many have passed over to the other side. Many have reached what the man of Avon called the "chair age." A few are still in the vigor of life. All passed through a life's experience such as will come to no other people. They all played a part in that grand drama which closed the heroic epoch in politics and war. They watched, step by step, the political legislation, and the unfolding, like the bloom of the deadly night-shade, of the divergent sentiments among the people of the two great Sections. They saw the resulting partisan strife, of which Bourbon County was the storm-center, and the culmination in bloody civil war. They saw the primal cause—that exudation from the dark ages—go down forever on the very spot of its origin, "the Plantations on the river James." They saw the wayward sisters, as from a pathway through a burning forest, emerge into the sunlight. They saw civilization,—cradled on the rock of Sinai and crowned on the rock of Plymouth,—plant here another guidon under the rising battle-smoke of 1865.

THE END.

J. F. COTTRELL,

WHOLESALE AND RETAIL

BOOKSELLER,

Stationer

AND WALL PAPER DEALER,

No. 6 North Main Street,

First Door North of Opera House,

FORT SCOTT, KANSAS.

—ESTABLISHED 1865.—

T. L. Herbert,

DEALER IN POLISHED

Plate and Window Glass

WALL PAPER,

Window Shades, Paints, Oils and Varnish.

PAINTER AND PAPER HANGER.

207 Wall Street.

Established 1869.   Incorporated 1888.

W. H. STOUT, President.   R. J. HARRIS, Vice-Pres't.   W. H. FOX, Sec. & Treas.

THE FORT SCOTT

GRAIN & IMPLEMENT COMPANY

(Successors to DURKEE & STOUT,)

Agricultural Implements,

CARRIAGES, BUGGIES,

GRAIN AND SEEDS.

FORT SCOTT,   -   KANSAS.

JOHN GLUNZ,

WHOLESALE DEALER IN

LEATHER, ※ SADDLERY ※ HARDWARE,

Saddlery, Shoe Leather and Finding.

Manufacturer of　　　　　　　　117 MARKET ST.,
HORSE COLLARS. HIDES. FORT SCOTT, KANSAS.

W. B. Hunter,
PRESCRIPTION DRUGGIST,

AND Manufacturer of Well Known

Pharmaceutical Preparations and Proprietary Remedies.

ALSO, A FULL LINE OF

DRUGS, CHEMICALS,

Perfumery and Toilet Articles of Every Description, and Physicians' Supplies.

Corner Main and Wall Streets,
　　　　　　　　FORT SCOTT, KANSAS.

FORT SCOTT FURNITURE COMPANY.

Nos. 10, 12 and 14 Scott Avenue.

Furniture & Undertaking.

Carrying the Largest and Best Selected Stock of

MEDIUM AND HIGH GRADE FURNITURE

In this Section. Buying all goods in car load lots for CASH enables us to undersell all competitors. We can sell Furniture at same price it costs small dealers, and Guarantee to Save You at Least 20 per Cent.

 ## UNDERTAKING DEPARTMENT.

* * * *

Scientific Embalming.

COFFINS AND CASKETS,

Iron, Metallic, Copper and Zinc.

SHROUDS, ROBES, Etc.

A complete equipment of Hearses, Pall Bearers' Wagonette, Carriages, Hacks and Undertaker's Wagons.

No Extra Charge for Hearses in the Country,

This Department is under the direct supervision of C. W. Goodlander, Jr.,—18 years practical experience in this city and adjacent territory.

CHAN. B. CAMPBELL,

Insurance

AND Loans....

FIRE, LIGHTNING, CYCLONE, HAIL, WIND STORM, PLATE GLASS, LIFE AND ACCIDENT.

All classes of Insurance at equitable rates.
Loans promptly made on Farm and City Property.
All kinds of Conveyancing and Notarial work done.
Rents collected and properties cared for.

Call and see me when you want business in my line.

FORT SCOTT, KANSAS.

D. PRAGER,

Watches,

and Jewelry,

UNION BLOCK.

No. 18 Main Street, - FORT SCOTT, KANSAS.

C. C. NELSON.　　　　　　　　　　　　　　　W. P. SMITH.

C. C. NELSON & CO.,
LOANS.

Loans Promptly Negotiated on Farm and City Property.

Low Rates of Interest and Easy Payments on Principal.

Office: 112 E. First Street,　　　　FORT SCOTT, KANSAS.

J. V. DABBS,

The Old Reliable

Photographer,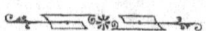

GROUND FLOOR STUDIO.

New Process Portraits, Crayon Portraits,
　　　　Water Colored Portraits, Frames and Mouldings,
　　　　　　　　Colored Pictures, Photogravures.

207 Market Street,　- -　FORT SCOTT, KANSAS.

1858.   1894.
Pioneer Lumber Yard

C. W. GOODLANDER,
......DEALER IN......

Lumber and Grain,

Sash, Doors, Blinds, Cement, Lime and
======All Kines of Building Material.

YARDS AND ELEVATORS.
Fort Scott, Kansas, Arcadia, Kansas, Uniontown, Kansas, Garland, Kansas, Bronson, Kansas, Liberal, Mo.

T. W. LYNN, Manager.

W. A. COSTON,
Dentist,
No. 103 SOUTH MAIN STREET,
FORT SCOTT,
KANSAS.

H. L. PAGE AND CO.
DEALERS IN
ALL KINDS OF VEHICLES.

They buy direct from the manufacturers, therefore are able and do give their customers the benefit of as low prices on all the different grades and styles of vehicles, as can be had of any dealer in the State. They carry a large stock of

Spring Wagons, Phaetons, Buggies, Road Wagons.

Also, a fine line of **Harness.** They sell the celebrated BAIN WAGON.

Their long experience enables them to select from the different factories the best articles made for Farm Machinery. Their NEW IDEAL MOWER, with ball and roller bearing journals, serrated ledger plates, is without doubt the best Mower now made.

The New Deering Pony Binder, With ball and roller bearing.

No. 1 Market Square,   **FORT SCOTT, KANASS.**

Warn Hardware Co.,
DEALERS IN
HARDWARE,
Cutlery, Stoves and Tinware,
21 SOUTH MAIN STREET.

AGENTS FOR FAVORITE STOVES AND RANGES,

The most durable, convenient, economical and best operating Stoves and Ranges sold in this city or county.

1871. 1894.

H. BROWN,

Merchant Tailor.

FINE TAILORING A SPECIALTY.

NO. 211 MARKET STREET,

Fort Scott, - Kansas.

T. W. Tallman Lumber Company,

DEALERS IN

 **LUMBER,**

New and Complete Stock of Builders' and Plasterers' Material Always on Hand.

Yards, Cor. National Ave. and Third St., Opposite Court House,

FORT SCOTT, KANS.

1870.  1894.

OFFICE OF THE

Fort Scott Marble and Granite Works,

Cor. Third and  **M. E. FARNSWORTH,**
Main Streets. **Proprietor.**

Dealer in Quincy, Barre, Clark's Island, Oak Hill, Hallowell, Concord, Black Diamond, Red Beach and Bay of Fundy Granites. Importer of Scotch Granite, Statuary Figures, Italian Marble and Finished Monuments.

CORRESPONDING OFFICES:
Aberdeen, Scotland, . . . and . . . Carrara, Italy.

All communications should be addressed
and remittances made to **I. W. MOODY, Manager.**
All parties desiring work in our line would do well to call and see our stock and
GET OUR PRICES.

C. W. GOODLANDER, PRESIDENT.   C. H. OSBUN, VICE PRES'T.   C. B. McDONALD, CASHIER.

ORGANIZED IN 1884.

Citizens National Bank.

PAID UP CAPITAL, $100,000.   AUTHORIZED CAPITAL, $300,000.

Directors. T. W. Tallman, G. W. Katzung, W. P. Dilworth, C. W. Goodlander, C. H. Osbun, F. M. Brickley, B. P. McDonald, Leo I. Stadden, W. C. Perry.

Bank on Main Street, FORT SCOTT, KANSAS.

Goodsell, Calhoun & Co.,

DRY GOODS, NOTIONS, KID GLOVES, CLOAKS,

Complete Line of Seasonable Goods
AT ALL TIMES,
Can be Found at our Store.

GOODSELL, CALHOUN & CO.

DAVID F. COON,	J. J. STEWART,	JAS. R. COLEAN,
PRESIDENT.	VICE PRESIDENT.	CASHIER,

The State Bank,

COR. OF MAIN AND FIRST STREETS,

FORT SCOTT, KANSAS.

Capital, - - - $100,000.

DIRECTORS.

C. H. Haynes,	C. C. Crain,	J. J. Stewart,
John H. Mead,	Thornton Ware,	D. F. Coon,
W. H. Harris,	Henry J. Butler,	Jas. R. Colean.

C. E. HALL,

Druggist,

FORT SCOTT, KANS.

The Best is the Cheapest!

Prescriptions Filled at all hours: Day or Night.

Quality Pays!

We handle only reliable goods of the best makes, and sell them at prices as low as may be consistent with good quality.

TOILET ARTICLES, PERFUMES, BRUSHES, COMBS, MIRRORS.

C. E. HALL, Druggist,
...112 S. MAIN STREET....

www.ingramcontent.com/pod-product-compliance
Lightning Source LLC
Chambersburg PA
CBHW070246230426
43664CB00014B/2416